LEAVES

ESCAPING RELIGION   DISCOVERING GRACE

KURT BLOMBACK

Please note that the NIV was revised in 2011 with some minor tweaks, so if you look up a reference online you might not get an exact match. I read and studied the 1984 for over 40 years. Kind of hard to switch.

This is a work of non-fiction, all stories are based on true events, names may have been changed in some cases. It is not intended to be a precise record of events and theology, but rather a commentary on personal understanding of the Bible.

Cover design by Elizabeth Blomback using Canva®

Back cover photo by Daniel Lombardi, climber Ryan Blomback.

ISBN 9798344395456

For the kids

In Memory of Paul Shiffer

1956-2011

TABLE OF CONTENTS

THE THANKS

I view myself as the product of other people's prayers and to the hundreds of fellow believers that God has used to guide me through life, I am very grateful. Pastors, Nav Staff, Bible study leaders, friends, missionaries, fellow Marines and fellow citizens of God's Kingdom, all have been instrumental in my life.

A special shout out to my test readers who provided valuable feedback as the book emerged and to Buck Turgison MD who made sure the medical facts were correct with "The Game". BTW he was also my roommate at that time. The Butterman and the Vance, fellow Marine Officers. My early Navigator staff, Jim Payton and John Robinson and of course the Soup, who taught me so much about so many things.

My final proof readers: my wife Linda and my favorite daughter in law, Liz, were invaluable in transforming a ranting manifesto into something readable. Correcting a myriad of punctuation, capitalization and verb tenses takes a lot of time and attention. This is definitely outside of my abilities.

I wrote this book by mistake. My youngest aspired to be a writer so I undertook this project to connect with my kid. The child has since abandoned the goal but I found that I could not stop writing, so I completed the project. I found it to be a magnificent means to meditate on a Biblical theme and that, justified the endeavor. Publishing allows the opportunity to possibly help others, so into the world of self-publishing I leap.

My highest gratitude goes to my wife who has lived a life of grace with me for some 36 years. Fig Leaves would not be in your hands without her contributions, example and support.

THE INTRO

My story is similar to the prodigal son found in Luke 15. Desperate circumstances caused me to turn to God. The wayward son and I both surrendered to the idea that this would require taking on the role of a lowly servant, an appropriate penance for our errant ways and a means to appease a disappointed God. Such an arrangement would be far from ideal but it remained several steps up from where we were, thus the choice was clear.

But the grace and love of the Father was so much more than either one of us fathomed. The fatted calf on the BBQ, a celebration of the angels, a royal robe bestowed on our shoulders and the full rights and privileges of a son restored. Who would have thought that we would be welcomed home like this. Who would have thought we were this valuable and cherished? The Scriptures, however are quite clear; that this is indeed the case. Stumbling into the marvelous reality of the Gospel, it would take decades to fully appreciate what transpired on the day I laid my life at the foot of the cross.

There is so much rumor theology these days that misrepresents what the Bible is really all about. It took me too many years to untangle truth from error. So many popular ideas fall apart in light of verses that are just plain and simple to understand. Too much time was wasted following popular dead ends. I invite you to invest a little bit of time and "come and see" what it is all about....you will not be disappointed.

My prayer is a simple; "God, show my readers your love, show them your amazing grace".

I am but a bird dog that points to a great reality. I hope to start people thinking about a life-altering truth and hope that folks will base their lives on the amazing grace of God revealed in the Scriptures.

THE BIG PICTURE

The days of my youth are far behind me now, but there remain a few precious memories that have survived the purging of time. I deeply long to relive such days when I was truly alive in every sense of the word. Despite the passing of so many years, I can still recall the aroma of sweat, climbing chalk and just a hint of blood on just such a day in the Mojave Desert of California. Visibility was truly unlimited, perhaps pushing 100 miles as the clear blue sky was completely void of anything resembling a cloud.

My climbing partner Vance and I paused as we reveled in the experience that few drink in; the summit. To the climbers that read this I need not explain, but we marveled at how there can be a drug problem in America when there is rock climbing. The feet of very few have stood on top of this summit. The breadth and scope of the landscape was fully in view. The perspective, the endorphins, the sense of achievement were the exhilarating rewards for the day. Skillful use of carabiners, ropes, nuts and knots with just a pinch of bravado thrown in, got us to the top.

Thus, we got to treat our eyes to the 360-degree grandeur before us. Granola bars and tepid water were culinary delights as we kicked back and enjoyed a well-deserved rest upon the summit. We dwelled in this perfect moment for quite some time, enjoying it immensely. Unfortunately, after a while, the realities of life's timetable slowly crept in; a long drive home, to do lists, jobs and the hankering for a well-deserved cheeseburger took over, and it was time to descend. We peeled the athletic tape from our fingers with our teeth as we readied ourselves to rappel back into the world of ordinary people. Then we both noticed an eco-tourist driving through the park, taking snapshots from the comfort of an air-conditioned minivan. We exchanged glances, and shook our heads in disbelief, our thoughts were obvious to each other…they just didn't get it, they were missing so much, they were missing the big picture.

The best of my climbing days are well behind me now, but the mountains around my home in Montana allow me on their tops a few times a year. The routes I take are less steep and rarely involve ropes, but the peaks still beckon, and I heed their call from time to time. The enormity of the Rocky Mountains deeply moves my soul, as does the solitude of the summit. Yes, it is addictive, I enjoy it immensely. I make no apology for this indulgence, and in a way, it is analogous to a perspective I have after crawling with God for 40+ years. I see the big picture and where I came from and how most people are missing so much about life. Please allow me to share my story about my arduous climb that enabled me to escape religion and walk with the risen Christ in a Spirit-to-spirit relationship, the foundational relationship that is the very reason we were created. The bedrock of this story revolves around an often undiscovered but central truth called grace.

My journey starts in the Catskill Mountains of New York. It was there, as a confused unbelieving teenager, I prayed from my soul for the very first time. It was a cry for help. In the clarity of retrospect, it became obvious, that God answered my prayer in a truly magnificent way, but at the time, there was simply no reply, only a troubling silence. Unbeknownst to me, God started to order and arrange the circumstances in my life so, when the silence was broken years later at the cross, my eyes became wide open and I got a life changing glimpse of His incomprehensible love, His absolute and total forgiveness and His offer of real life. My response was the only appropriate one; I responded with the totality of my being. Abandoning my life as I knew it, I embarked on a journey of faith; I became a follower of Jesus, a servant of the Risen Christ, the very Son of God became my Lord, Savior and Teacher. My life started over; I was, as the Bible depicts: born again[1].

Shortly thereafter, a long tedious climb began. God's agenda was to systematically deprogram my mind, in order to lift me out of the depths of a self-made righteousness to a real righteousness that is by faith. The summit is a grace-based relationship with God. This is in direct contrast to the error of religion where it is thought that rules and performance can actually qualify us for God's approval and eternal life; they don't. The climb is against the ever-present gravity of religion's delusion, it is a powerful force that constantly wants to dash me on the rocks below. Slips and falls are the norm on such a climb but tied into His grace I am consistently caught. Dinged but not damaged, and at times hanging upside down and spinning at the end of my rope. My Guide gets me back onto the route toward the summit. Decades later, I am still not even close to the summit but I am indeed above the tree line and the view is magnificent.

There are two theologies that battle for the souls of people. This battle has been going on for thousands of years. Am I accepted by God because of <u>my</u> goodness (religion) or am I accepted by God because of <u>His</u> goodness (grace)? What I do versus what He did, who I am vs who He is. Not a minor detail, but rather polar opposites with enormous consequences.

The erroneous rumor theology of a righteousness by works has been so prevalent throughout history and in virtually every major religion, that it seems to pass as unquestioned truth. The scope of this error is best described as pandemic, one must be diligent to avoid this trap.

Works righteousness, the law, religion and other labels describe a theology that is actually the default setting of people. Religion, or our

---

[1] John 3:3

effort, our solution, is symbolized by the familiar fig leaves of Eden. It is the very first thing Adam and Eve do right after the fall. Yet despite its popularity, religion is a game where even if you "win" you lose. We will explore this in detail in the coming chapters but suffice it to say, for now, the only play is to not participate.

Religion is the toxin that causes great harm to both believer and unbeliever, it is a lie that damages every relationship we have. But the reason we believe it is indicative of an even deeper problem. Fig leaves are a symptom of faith in self, rather than faith in God. When we see this Achilles heel of self-supremacy in people, everything in the Scriptures seems to transform from a collection of odd stories to a cohesive narrative. Every pain we observe in life, can be understood in light of this fatal flaw of humans: pride.

However, God does not abandon us to our fate. Within the first few pages of the Bible, we see that the stage is set for a drama that will right this wrong. The grand drama that we follow is the battle of religion vs the cross, "Fig Leaves" is the title of the play. Cain and Abel, Isaac and Ishmael, Jacob and Esau, David and Saul, Jesus and the Pharisees, Paul and the circumcision group, all are players in this Biblical battle between the two theologies that has gone on for thousands of years. The core message of this Biblical drama is called the "Gospel". It is the Greek word for "good news". The Gospel reveals a God that will rescue us and restore us, for the reality is that we cannot accomplish this by ourselves. The hero of this drama will be Jesus, not us. Humbling as this may be, it remains the key to our rescue.

Our pride, our self-supremacy caused our destruction. Religion, ultimately rooted in this pride, doesn't solve anything, it simply locks us into our demise. Conversely, humility and the supremacy of Christ, reverses everything and puts us on a path of restoration and the path to the summit, the original master plan for our existence.

Thousands of years ago the wisest man ever, had this figured out. Solomon pegged the big picture when he saw that all of humanity fell into two camps; the proud and the humble. How God subsequently deals with these two groups is really quite simple. James, the brother of Jesus, requotes Solomon with the concise axiom.;

"God opposes the proud, but gives grace to the humble"[2]

Pride, the lowest common denominator, is the root cause of all our turmoil, alienation and pain. Pride and religion we will find go hand in hand. Conversely, humility and the cross are the keys for both healing and eternal life. Discovering Biblical grace is the catalyst for escaping the quick sands of religion and becoming more like a mountain goat dancing on the solid rock of the summit, or as the Prophet Habakkuk pens:

"The Lord my Lord is my strength; he makes my feet like those of a deer and enables me to walk on mountain heights!"[3]

Spoiler alert:

This is not a self-help book. My big picture perspective is not the result of me overcoming and figuring out life. I did not overcome any obstacles here by myself. I am simply writing from the perspective of someone who has been rescued. 2000 years ago, God's Son died on a cross. The power of this event, poorly understood by most, still retains an incredible life altering potential. It can reconnect us with our Heavenly Father, which is nothing short of life changing and eternity shifting.

I accidentally stumbled into this marvelous reality 40+ years ago. A prayer of desperation in the Catskill Mountains started it all. But the power of the Gospel is just as effective today as it was 2000 years ago. I know this for certain and from this experience, truly alive and reborn I write. There are not any original thoughts in this book, I simply have repackaged the truth of the Bible and personalized it. For this deliverance I take no credit at all. It was not my moral resolve, my intellect, nor skill, it was rather, by God's truth. I am simply passing on the whispered secret on how to escape the prison of self.

---

[2] James 4:6

[3] Habakkuk 3:19 CSB, see also Psalm 18:33

The chronology of my journey will be a bit scrambled as we jump back and forth on the timeline. This is because I arranged chapters by progressive concept instead of chronological sequence for easier understanding. This helps the majority of folks who are linear thinkers. So, walk with me for a bit and brace yourself for some raw theology and a touch of deadpan humor. Perhaps a thing or two I learned will assist you in grasping the big picture ...

We will start our journey in a small boat rocking gently in the Great South Bay of Long Island, New York. We will learn about the Gospel from a fish. From there we will follow me to college in upstate New York where I get saved, then to the US Marine Corps, where as an Infantry Officer, God teaches me many things, then to Montana where I now live, learn, write and grow old.

Well, let us see what we can learn from a fish....

THE FLOUNDER

I cannot imagine that the flounder is an extremely intelligent fish. After all, we had a few dozen of them flopping around in the bottom of our boat. Their brains are about the size of a pea and are no match for the intellect of a human. But such is the fate of those that are lower on the food chain. The salt, the gulls, the telltale tug on the line, all are part of a successful day of fishing, and a great introduction to the greatest story of all; The Gospel.

Being at the top of the food chain, we rarely contemplate what goes through the mind of the lowly flounder. One minute they are living the life of ease in the Great South Bay, then, before they know it, something has gone very wrong and they are ripped out of their world, literally a fish out of water and tossed into the bottom of a boat. Their new world is full of strange sounds and sights, nothing seems to work. The hull of the boat is now the walls of their new prison. An appropriate sense of doom looms. We can imagine them conversing amongst themselves, "How did we get here?" The answer, "One wrong bite", "one wrong decision".

The Genesis story is virtually identical, Adam fell for the bait and like the flounder, Adam did not understand the consequences of the hook. God was quite clear to Adam and Woman;[4] eat anything in the garden except for the "tree of the knowledge of good and evil…or you surely die."[5] God painted the big picture for Adam, "eat and die". Satan, of course, only shows one side of the ledger when tempting, the side that does not have the hook, nor the frying pan.

For some reason we seem to get caught up in the details about whether it was an apple or a pomegranate or perhaps a fig. This is totally irrelevant. The thrust of the passage is not about fruit, it's about grasping the idea that one wrong decision can have catastrophic consequences. So, let's break down the events of Eden, as we explore the prelude of the Gospel, which is known as "the fall": the bad news before the good.

The original audience of Genesis was a bit more poetic and used stories and symbols to teach moral lessons. God connected to these folks and set up the scene in the garden as such, but as scientific Americans, with an obsession for chronological precision and cause and effect, we struggle with the creation account in Chapters 1 and 2. Our brains scream for answers: When? How? Thus, we miss the focus of the passage; who did it and why? People were created by God to bear his image[6] and to love Him and love others who were also created in his image. Love God and love people, this is the relational world that we were created for, this is our ocean, this is our natural realm, this is where we function correctly, this is where we belong.

My degree is in zoology so from time to time I enjoy asking the question, "What separates people from the animals"? I spent four years studying animals, so I feel somewhat qualified to guide this discussion. I let the conversation play out a bit because few people

---

[4] "Woman" was Eve's original name, it got changed to Eve after the fall, Genesis 2:23 & 3:20

[5] Genesis 2:17

[6] Genesis 1:26

contemplate such things these days and, to be fair, the answer is complex and multifaceted. Let's not focus on the metaphysical concepts like self-awareness or the philosophical "I think, therefore, I am" nonsense. Let's look at the everyday stuff, the observables, things like a phonetic alphabet, currency, power tools, funerals and of course toilet paper. All indeed are unique behaviors amongst Homo sapiens but what I am ultimately fishing for (pun intended) are two behaviors never observed in any animal: religion and clothes.

We remain hard wired in the fabric of our being to have a relationship with God and one would be hard pressed to find a time in history or a place in geography where some form of religion is not found. Being created in the image of our heavenly Father, it's easy to conclude that we are His kids. A healthy relationship with our Heavenly Father is paramount to our existence, it is in fact, the very core of our being. It doesn't take an Einstein to figure out that kids are supposed to dwell in the house of their Father.

We have lost this connection to God, but the compelling need to know Him stubbornly remains and this massive hole in our souls drives this unique behavior called religion. The common misguided themes in all religions, seems to be, "what do we have to do to get God's approval?" We ask this question because we are irresistibly driven by our subconscious to conclude that we do not have it.

Strip a person of his or her clothes and we feel ashamed and embarrassed; our confidence shattered, we scramble to cover ourselves with the nearest thing: a towel, a pillow, anything. Need proof of that? Ask anyone if they like hospital gowns. Those infernal things were created by someone that seems to get pleasure in degrading people's dignity when they need it the most. In Adam's case, when he realized he was buck naked he grabbed fig leaves. We, likewise, scramble to cover our souls with the first thing that appears to hide our shame: a righteousness by works. Handy and nearby, religion or what we do, appears to work from our perspective. Our shame seems to be covered, the problem seems solved, but innately we know that the fig leaves of performance are worthless before God. When God nears, we run and hide. Our efforts to fix things have gone horribly awry.

Enter the serpent.

Biblical scholars, of whom I am not, seem to boil down "the tree of knowledge of good and evil" as symbolic of one of two things. The first idea is that we elevate ourselves above God's commands and choose to obey or not obey. The second school of thought seems to be along the lines that we define our own morality, man-made definitions of right and wrong.

Simpleton me, a mere electrician, I find the common denominator in both, to be supremacy of self. I would, in fact, go one step further and propose that it is a case of "self-lord" or "self-god". The role of who decides what is best quietly shifts to self. God is kicked off the throne as we take His place. The Snake was right, this does feel good, it's kind of fun, I can get used to this. Note the key point of temptation by the serpent, "You will be like God…[7]". The best lies are the ones that are true. Yes, you can be the supreme being in your life, you can sit on the throne and be like God, and have the final say, but the cost is enormous.

The worm of self with the hidden hook is dangled before us and we took the bait. This course of action seemed to be a great idea at the time, it makes total sense, but like the flounder, mesmerized by the bait before him, the fallacy of trusting in self rather than God is unseen. The end game will be completely catastrophic. So, like a fish out of water, gasping for life, we are people disconnected from our life-giving Father, gasping for spiritual life, gasping for that breath of God that made us alive in Eden. We have been yanked from the realm that we were created to live in, not the physical realm but rather the spiritual realm where we naturally and selflessly love God and love people.

This trap of self is relationally toxic and spiritually lethal. Unless someone punches a hole through the boat's hull, our destiny will be sealed, the clock ticks, we need to be rescued, because it is impossible to save ourselves.

This self-lord, self-savior, which is ultimately symptoms of faith in self, is what the Bible calls "pride". It is simply the condition where self has

---

[7] Genesis 3:5

become the supreme being in our lives and this is the relational systemic toxin that destroys our relationship with God and our relationships with other people. It is the ultimate cause for spiritual death and is the essence of our spiritual prison.

The opposite of pride is humility, which manifests itself by faith in God as Savior and Lord. A theological leap, in light of the New Testament and the Father handing the kingdom over to his Son, the correct line, would be faith in Jesus as both Lord and Savior. Lord Self or Lord Jesus? A singular decision with enormous and eternal consequences. Flip the switch one way and we get darkness and death, flip the switch the other way and we get light and life. Pride verses humility. Once again, James states the obvious.

"God opposes the proud but gives grace to the humble"[8]

Some argue, "How can we be accountable for Adam's sin?" This is truly an academic exercise in futility for we all made this decision. Fueled by pride, we dethrone God and put ourselves in God's rightful place. We decide to obey or create our own sense of morality every day. Adam was merely the climber at the top of the mountain that triggered the avalanche. Today, billions continue in this pattern and the full force of the avalanche leaves a path of utter destruction through all of history. Disagree? I would point you to today's news feed, full of pain, death and destruction. God was clearly right, "eat and die". Pride is ultimately the source of our cataclysmic course. For millennia we have tried to fix it by our own efforts and the hope of resolution seems ever elusive; our effort, our design, our solution, our reliance on ourselves are our fig leaves. We got ourselves into this mess, relying on ourselves to get out only gets us deeper. Like fish flopping in the bottom of a boat, our efforts just injure ourselves and others and ultimately wear ourselves out. We must stop pursuing this obviously dead end.

---

[8] James 4:6 NIV 1984

Enter the Good News.

There is, however, a hole punched through the bottom of the boat, it is the cross. This is our escape route back to our ocean. We can be restored to the world we were created for if we respond to the finished work of the cross with humility, faith and repentance. I will confess that my humility, faith, and repentance was woefully incomplete at first, but God honors even the simplest mustard seed of faith. Redeemed and reconciled at the instant of faith (justification), restoration is what follows and is more of a process of detoxification (sanctification). Dying to self and pride and trusting more and more in the depths of God's incredible love and grace, in what seems like an excruciating slow process, my sanctification has begun. I still have a long road ahead but at least I can breathe, and the terror of living a life apart from God is only a memory of long ago.

However, I am getting ahead of myself, so let's downshift and examine the Fall of people in a bit more detail as explained in the Book of Beginnings, Genesis. What went wrong with our connection to God and how is it fixed? The flounder has helped us wrap our brain around a few things so let's see what a squirrel can show us.

THE SQUIRREL

As a young man growing up amongst the oak forests and drumlins of Long Island, I learned the ways of the grey squirrel. Acorns were to be had by the bucket load and squirrels, likewise, were in abundance. From time to time we hunted them and we had it down to a science.

Squirrels are absolute masters of the arboreal. Climbing with ease and making incredible leaps from tree to tree at impressive heights. These aerial acrobats seek safety in the tree tops whenever they feel threatened. A dog or cat would appear, and the little rascal would scurry up the nearest tree, all of which they seemed to have memorized. Safe in the tree they seemed to mock their opponents with a telltale bark, and to warn fellow squirrels that there were games afoot. Their main play was to hide behind the trunk of a tree. Mr. Squirrel would depend on keeping the trunk of the tree between you and him and wait for you to walk on by. But therein lies his fatal flaw, the squirrel hunter knows this and uses this to his advantage. The game is all but over, in a few moments his quarry will be in the bag. You see the hunter sends his partner to the other side of the tree while he readies his trusty rifle. Mr. Squirrel, not being a rocket scientist and unable to count, quickly scurries to the opposite side where the first hunter awaits. In his sights, the game is over.

Let's not be hasty and think the squirrel is a fool because, likewise, we fall for the same trick every time. We have faith in self and in our self-reliance, we try to solve our sin problem with the fig leaves of good works and into the sights of our enemy we go. We play a game that we cannot win. Blinded by our depravity, we are convinced that we cannot lose. We endlessly repeat the same mistake of works righteousness over and over again. We are driven by pride and into the vortex of religion we are pulled. The "winners" are the Pharisees[9], religious extremists, who are enemies of grace. The losers are "sinners", crippled by debilitating guilt and paralyzing inferiority. Crushed by the master accuser, Satan, and those that do his work: physical, social and spiritual bullies. Both the crushers and the crushed play the same game: steal and kill and destroy[10] is all the enemy knows.

Enter the fig leaves.

Right after Adam and Woman sin, she looks at Adam and giggles and points, "Hey your package is hanging out". Adam turns beet red and retorts, "Look who is flapping in the breeze[11]". "Houston, we have a problem", we realize we are naked and ashamed and what follows seems to be the default "go to" solution repeated a bazillions times in history, we solve the problem. Yes, to be absolutely clear, the problem is that Adam and Eve solved the problem[12]. I will pause for a moment because you probably had to read that twice. The very premise of this book is that we get into trouble because we attempt to solve the problem of sin; this is religion, this is works righteousness, expedient but very wrong. Let's walk through this slowly and very carefully.

Americans vapor lock on this passage because as a free people we are pioneers, innovators and entrepreneurs, we thrive on problem

---

[9] Pharisees were the religious leaders in Biblical times

[10] John 10:10

[11] I am paraphrasing Genesis 3:7 here

[12] My paraphrase of Genesis 3:7

solving. We built transcontinental railroads, we cured diseases, we pioneered flight, dug the Panama Canal, we invented the lightbulb, hey, we even put man on the moon with our problem solving. How in the world could solving the problem be the problem? The key point here is understanding that <u>who</u> provides the solution is the issue at hand. Let's look at Genesis Chapter 3 again and recap.

Their new self-supremacy caused people to sin and created a problem of being naked and ashamed. Then, keeping in step with pride, they sewed fig leaves together to solve the problem. This is self-reliance or more theologically correct; self-sufficiency[13], an obvious extension of self-supremacy and pride. It is important to understand that from their depraved perspective this appeared to work, they looked down and their package was covered, mission accomplished or so they thought (self-deception). I will introduce the idea at this time that the real issue was not fig leaves at all, but rather fig leaves poetically represents the real problem, which is faith in the new supreme being in their lives, faith in self. The Bible calls this self-supremacy, self-reliance and self-deception; pride.

Worldwide and throughout history fig leaves of religion dominate. They appear to work, and we convince ourselves and others that this is what we should do. But like snake oil salesmen, the claims are empty. Humanity lines up for the lie, "If I only do____(Fill in the blank), God will love me and reward me with eternal life". Scrambling to cover our nakedness and in some way fill the hole in our souls, we gorge ourselves on this sweet tasting poison that tickles our pride. Unfortunately, this mindset actually makes the problem much worse. As such, Adam did not solve their problem but the pattern here is the key take away. We follow in lock step and we do exactly the same thing and repeat the error. Who provides the solution, is the thrust of Genesis 3, man or God…let's continue.

---

[13] We are going to use the term "self reliance" henceforth, since this resonates with most people

Enter God.

Now it is appropriate to note who is seeking who. God is seeking Adam and although Adam is clothed in his new fig leaves, he is afraid and hiding[14]. Adam's hiding points us to how his understanding of God has gone terribly wrong. This is a key dimension of what theologians call "the depravity of man". Cut off from God we can no longer think correctly. It is nothing short of lunacy to play hide and seek with an omniscient God; you simply lose every time. But Adam, nevertheless, attempts it. God is not fooled for a moment. But this, "who is seeking who" comes into play in the New Testament when Jesus says that, "He comes to seek and save what was lost[15]" and I can affirm this and testify that He came seeking me after my Catskill prayer of "Where are you?".

"So, what's with the fig leaves?" God asks, playing dumb for dramatic purposes.

"She made me do it.", replies Adam, as the first blame shift in history rears its ugly head.

"The Devil made me do it" immediately follows as the Woman also catches on to this feel-good blame game[16].

Like Adam, we know that our solutions do not solve anything, so we are insecure before God. We seek to shed as much blame as possible by blaming our failures on others. Fig leaves appear to work as we compare ourselves to others, but they become clearly inadequate in front of God. All of our actions, our good works, our faith in self, fool others and even ourselves, but they completely fall apart before a holy God. Fig leaves are a product of a self-savior. It is abundantly clear from the Scriptures that our efforts are worthless.

Our brains are usually numb half way through chapter 3 and don't start functioning again until Cain kills Abel in chapter 4, so we miss the best

---

[14] Genesis 3:8-13

[15] Luke 19:10

[16] Genesis 3:12-13 paraphrased

part. God provides a solution by providing clothes made from animal skins[17]. Four crucial points about grace are introduced here.

First, blood, which represents life[18], must be paid in order to deal with the problem of sin. The scales of justice can be balanced by an exchange of life for death. The Bible in the first few pages, subtly introduces the plot line that blood is the currency of atonement[19]. Bible commentators call this recurring theme, "The Scarlet Thread[20]". This is one of the earliest foreshadowing of Christ's role as the Messian. It helps us identify Jesus as the Perfect Priest, that will offer the Perfect Sacrifice, that is the Perfect Solution to make people perfect. It must also be noted that the blood is not ours.

Second, God must provide the solution to the problem of sin; not us. Anything other than the finished work of the cross is a fig leaf and worthless.

Third, it should be obvious that God's unconditional love for us is not lost due to sin.

Fourth, we must choose to take off our fig leaves of self-effort and embrace God's solution to the problem. We must stop this faith in self nonsense and choose to have faith in Christ. This is called repentance. Reversing trust in self to trusting in the rescuer, the Messiah.

Confidence in self and our solutions is a symptom of pride, but remember, "God opposes the proud but gives grace to the humble". The tree of life is cut off from us until we get this right. This is what awaits believers at the end of the Bible in Revelation. The finished work of the cross is the only way of to get us back to where we belong.

Satan appeals to our faith in self and pride repeatedly because this trick works so perfectly, like the go-to trick of the squirrel hunter, it is

---

[17] Genesis 3:21

[18] Leviticus 17:11

[19] Leviticus 17:11

[20] Or The Scarlett Cord see Joshua 2:17-18

page one of the enemy's play book and rarely does he have to turn the page. I will submit to you that Biblical pride is not the bragging, stubborn, self-important people that comes to mind when we hear the word, but rather someone who simply relies on his or her effort, an unmistakable symptom of self-supremacy and self-reliance. This pride or works righteousness always has one of two outcomes; self-righteousness or self-condemnation, both are a losing hand in this game. Legalism or works righteousness is a game we simply cannot win. The hallmark of both schools of thought is very simple to spot; comparison. Legalism is reliance on a moral code and is always evidenced by a comparative spirit[21];

This ideology is actually quite similar to the social construct of the popular crowd in high school. They self-define "cool" based on who they are, then project that standard onto everyone else. Thus, unleashing the venom of the snake; comparison. They look down on those not part of the "in" crowd. Those not included feel inferior. Many cave to peer pressure and conform, hoping to make the cut. The parallel to legalism should be clear. The self-spiritual and by extension, those that adhere to false religions, ultimately ride on a solution and course of action that is based on human effort. It doesn't matter if you make up your own rules or follow God's. Solutions based on performance are useless and are in direct conflict with God's perspective on the matter. Contempt and envy, bullying and peer pressure, the social battleground of high school, closely follows the spiritual battleground of adulthood.

Self-Righteous	**Self-Condemned**
I am better than them	I am such a loser
I am morally superior	I am a sinner
His sin is worse than mine	He is too perfect
Look at all the issues he has	I am so screwed up

21 Luke 18: 9-14

People love me because I am rich, fun and beautiful	If only I was rich, fun and beautiful people would love me
I find fault in others	I feel guilty
My problem is dependence on what I do	My problem is dependence on what I do

We ultimately rely on the supreme being in our lives for both lordship decisions and salvation. He is always our "go to" person for these things. There is little question in my mind that this is indeed the case. However, what we tell ourselves and others and what we truly believe, are usually entirely two different things. What we do is ultimately rooted in the reality of our belief system. We do what we do because we believe what we believe. Ultimately this will boil down to relying on the supremacy of Christ or relying on the supremacy of self. This relational toxin called pride wreaks havoc with our relationship with God and metastasizes to our relationship with people. It strikes at the very heart of our created purpose; "love God, love people".

Pride and self-supremacy are our default setting, but it generally shows itself in three basic ways. Remember self has taken the place of God in our lives and since Christ has three basic roles; Lord, Savior and Teacher, likewise these three expressions strike at the heart of one of the three roles of Christ. All three derail our created purpose to "love God and love people[22]". All three drive us further from our Father.

Rebellion

This expression is what we naturally define as sinful. Sex, drugs and rock and roll is the lifestyle of those that have rejected Christ as King. Self determines what the rules are and what is right and wrong. Self

---

[22] Matthew 22:38

also determines which of God's rules, if any, are valid and which are not. Adam eating the apple reveals that the final say is self.

Legalism

A broken connection to God is the result of disobedience and our shame is now obvious. However, instead of trusting God's solution to cover our shame, we rely entirely on our own ability for the fix. Our savior is self as we rely on what we do instead of God's forgiveness. Rigid adherence and wrong motives to both God's law and man-made rules are hallmarks of this displacement of Christ as Savior. A religious lifestyle is the modern-day equivalent of Adam's fig leaves.

Idolatry

Manufacturing a religion to your own specifications, or adhering to such, points to a person who has replaced Jesus as Teacher, the revealer of truth. Make up your own rules, whatever they may be, and create a false sense of security by creating the illusion of God's approval by all sorts of crazy self-created religions. Adam's confidence in his fig leaves and his playing hide and seek with an omniscient God indicates that our thinking has gone very wrong. All false religions are explained by this premise. All of the covenants revealed in Scripture are non-negotiated: God reveals, we respond. When we reverse this, we put ourselves in the driver seat. Adam does not perfect this, but his son Cain starts the ball rolling in the next chapter as false religion and murder are now part of the human condition

All three manifestations of sin are ultimately rooted in pride. Pride and self-supremacy are not only the source of spiritual death but also the continuance there of. All three reek of the stench of death, all three are disgusting to God, all three are diametrically opposed to our created purpose to bear the image of God, all three destroy us. Whichever poison you have chosen the solution is repentance and faith in the supremacy of Christ and formally declaring and practicing His role in our lives as Lord, Savior and Teacher[23].

My journey continues as the tables are turned between myself and the flounder. I come within seconds of drowning in a rip current off Fire Island, just a few miles from where I yanked flounders from the Great South Bay.

---

[23] Theologians formally refer to the three offices of Jesus as Prophet, Priest and King

THE RIP

The ocean waves were especially large that summer day in 1976, perhaps best described as dangerous. I was struggling with all my being to swim back to shore, but the rip current[24] did not care about my predicament. It was slowly and methodically dragging me out to the depths of the Atlantic. As each wave crashed, I must hold my breath for way too long as a wall of water washed over me. Normally, holding my breath for a long time is not a problem, but at the state of exhaustion I was in, those precious seconds of air were an absolute necessity. With each wave I seemed to lose ground in my struggle for air. I could see hundreds of people on the beach oblivious to my plight. The lifeguard equally clueless, was too busy watching bikinis. People were enjoying a beautiful summer's day at the beach, but my life in this high surf was measured in only seconds, I was drowning.

I was so exhausted and desperately gasping for air at that point that even a cry for help was impossible. The terror of drowning kicked in the adrenaline. I managed a few more feet towards shore as a lull in the intensity of the waves came. I flailed at the water as all manner of

---

[24] Rip currents account for most swimmer's death in the ocean

proper swim form was lost to panic and exhaustion. There was absolutely not a single thought in my brain except to get my feet on the precious shore that was only a stone's throw away. I was a young man of 15, my strength and skill were incapable of freeing myself from this powerful trap that gripped me. The inevitable came, I had nothing left. There is no possible win against the immense power of an ocean. Unable to fight the inescapable fatigue, I disappeared into the waves. However, in a most fortunate turn of events, a man noticed my peril and pulled me from the surf. I collapsed in utter exhaustion on the sand.

This sobering and terrifying episode in my life started an intense internal dialogue as I contemplated death seriously for the first time. I did not know anyone who had died and death was something one only read about in the newspapers or saw on TV. Death, a surreal concept, happened to other people, not me. I took a quantum leap in my comprehension of this reality that day. A deeply seated fear became embedded in my mind, one that would haunt me for years to follow; the fear of death.

The physical peril of that day closely paralleled my spiritual life. There was an immense force that was dragging me to destruction, it's called sin. My sin and the sin of others was going to swallow me up in a way that was utterly terrifying. Superficial people might have looked at me and thought I was a good kid; no drugs, no police, good in school, but deep down I was troubled and lost. Acceptance was something that eluded me and the more I tried, the more it backfired. My perspective of self-worth eroded at an alarming rate as my peers went from ignoring me to rejecting me, then ultimately as human vermin, to be crushed and discarded for their enjoyment. To ease this pain, I perfected the only defense mechanism at my disposal, I became cold and heartless, I withdrew from society and hated people. This defense mechanism was me clinging to a piece of flotsam as the rip current of sin carried me into a vast dark and lonely place. I became a bitter and pathological loner. Hundreds of onlookers were oblivious to my plight. They simply played while I was drowning, and there was absolutely nothing I could do to escape. As I drowned in life, I cried for help to an unseen God in the Catskill Mountains.

A few years later, a glimmer of hope presented itself. I was going to college hundreds of miles from my home. I saw an opportunity to escape my pain. The plan was simple: I could be anyone I wanted to be if no one really knew who I was. It seemed as though my identity was defined by others and if the people who knew me were not there, a new life could be attained. I certainly did not want to continue to live the way I was. In retrospect, the agony in my soul were the pangs of spiritual death. I was created to love God and love people, and, likewise feel loved by God and loved by people; I was zero out of four. God seemed like a million miles away. Cut off from God, I was biologically alive but spiritually dead, "unsaved" in the parlance of Christendom.

My eternal destiny was also unknown, and this was profoundly troubling. I looked at my good and my bad, deeply ingrained in my thought process was the meritocracy mindset. Was I good enough to get into heaven or were the fires of Hell my fate? Clearly my record was shoddy at best and my effort was far short. I simply could not do this. And like my alienation from people, it seemed like the more I tried to earn God's acceptance, the more I failed. Envisioning the judgment day of God, I had nothing. With the stakes as high as they get, uncertain is not the position to be in. One needs answers to this essential question, and I did not have a single clue, neither did anyone I knew, I was in a single word: lost.

My personality type is one of significant introversion. Relationships, though essential, are exhausting to me and, as a result, my relational illiteracy in my younger years was epic. My life seemed to be defined by this conundrum, needing friends but unable to make them. I didn't need an abundance of friends, but I did need a few of them. Relationally nimble people seem to be unable to understand this. They responded with contempt and, at times, verbal and physical attacks. This, of course, did not help me. These social bullies, drove me further from the friendships I needed, a vicious cycle. So I found solace in activities where I was away from people, backpacking was a perfect salve.

The Catskill Mountains were a convenient destination and also afforded a setting for reflection. Decompressed by the simplicity of the backpacking experience, the resulting clarity of mind caused me to confront a nagging intuition that I was supposed to be someone else. Likewise, I wrestled with “If you are a God of love, why is it so painful to be alive? Where are you? I’m drowning!” My life trajectory was dismal, and I was terrified by who I was. Something was very, very wrong here. God would answer this Catskill prayer in a few years, but first I had to be swept out to a sea of darkness.

At college in Oswego, New York I chose to major in zoology. I did not get along with people, but I seemed to do just fine with animals, so it seemed like a logical choice, besides it was fascinating. I intentionally tried to be someone else when I arrived. I tried my best to do the things that cool people did so I could be accepted by others, but my façade would not last, a couple months into this charade and my life completely imploded. People were as mean as before and the inescapable nightmare of rejection returned in full force and then some. My only defense was the familiar piece of flotsam that I clung to, the defense mechanism that defined me, I withdrew and once again, I became a bitter and angry loner.

This time it was different though, I shut off every bit of caring left inside of me and threw away the key, never ever to try this again. My heart now, irreversibly stone cold and dead, will no longer feel pain.[25] There are people that live lonely and bitter lives. I finally surrendered to the idea that I was going to be one of them. This is not who I wanted to be, but I was trapped by who I was, I knew nothing else. I found a solid grip on my flotsam and drifted into a black darkness. I disappeared and no one even noticed. I was in a very dark and lonely place and it seemed like no one was coming to rescue me because nobody even noticed that I vanished. Absolute and total despair; completely alone, biologically alive…spiritually dead. Like a flounder in the bottom of a boat, desperately gasping for life.

Like I have already mentioned, I liked activities that distracted me from my glaring disconnect from people and one of those coping

---

[25] For the record this does not work, I simply exchanged one problem for another

mechanisms was bicycle riding. I was actually quite good and invested in a very high-end bike. I would escape college on the weekends by cycling. A solo trip of over a hundred miles was not uncommon for me. I developed excellent stamina and became skilled at repairing my bicycle. God seems to work in mysterious ways, and this is a clear example of it. Like God seeking Adam in the garden, God was seeking me, in order to answer my prayer from years ago in the Catskill Mountains.

Across the hall in my dormitory was a fellow freshman named Mike. He was a decent guy, very outgoing and connected with me because he also had a bicycle and liked to ride. He, however, did not invest in a quality machine like I did and his bicycle seemed to be in need of constant repair. I found myself fixing his bicycle on a regular basis. This was my only tether to humanity, pathetic, I know, but that is where I was.

Enter the God Squad.

As time went on during my freshman year, I became aware of a group of Christians on my dorm floor known as the "God Squad". There were about a half a dozen of these so-called born-again Christians. They seemed compelled to "Spread the Word" and they connected with Mike, the bicycle guy, because he was an easy target with his outgoing personality. They had several conversations with him and he seemed intrigued by the topic. He, in turn, dragged me to one of these impromptu discussions one night. I was the withdrawn one that did not talk, but they got a lot of mileage out of Mike since he had the gift of gab. I overheard the Gospel being explained to someone else. Far from the perfect Gospel presentation, it was never the less, a spot of light in the darkness, the real possibility of a different life. One of the Christians noticed my attention.

Eating meals in both high school and college was a game I had to play ever so carefully. I timed my arrival to the cafeteria so that there would always be many empty tables so I could sit by myself. As I sat alone at an empty table one night eating my supper in the college dining hall that overlooked Lake Ontario, a member of the God Squad suddenly seats himself across the table from me.

"You're Kurt, right?" the Christian queried, as he mustered the courage to speak to a bitter person.

"Yeah" was my monosyllabic reply.

"We are showing a movie about the Bible[26] in my room tonight at 7. I want to invite you, because I think you will enjoy it".

"I'll think about it." was my guarded response.

"Well, I hope you come." were his parting words as he sensed awkward silence.

I made a simple and logical decision at that table that would dramatically alter the trajectory of my life. Every effort to earn a place in heaven was smeared by glaring faults in my life. My record was far from perfect. Also, every effort to become normal had catastrophically failed and the notion of death paralyzing. I was at absolute rock bottom. I have failed at life miserably. I had absolutely, positively, nothing to lose. So, I made the choice to invest time investigating this Bible option. If it was true, I would go for it; if it wasn't, then despair was the familiar life I had come to know. I might as well swim to this speck of light, or as Phillip prodded his friend Nathaniel, "Come and see[27]". I went to the movie. This decision in turn, led me to a more complete understanding of the Gospel.

My sins could be forgiven, all of them. God, who seemed like a million miles away, could dwell in my heart. Eternal life guaranteed. My head was spinning with these obvious truths. I sat at the base of a large ash tree a few days later and envisioned walking up to the cross at Calvary and planting my personal flag into the ground. "I now claim the death of Jesus as the payment for my sins. I now make Jesus the Lord of my life for the rest of my life. Please God, make me a new person from the inside out." With nothing to lose, this decision was absolute and irreversible. That night is permanently etched in my mind, its significance absolutely unparalleled, my life is clearly divided into two time periods based on that single night; before Christ and after.

---

[26] The movie was "What's Up Josh?" by Josh McDowell

[27] John 1:46

Understanding the cross is absolutely paramount to every human being. If you are not a believer, I urge you to make the same decision I did...seriously check it out. Grab the nearest Christian that you respect and demand that he or she explain this to you. Yes, you heard me right; DEMAND IT!

Clueless as I was to my new life, I took several days to ponder my new situation. It seemed like I needed to reveal my decision to the God Squad. The leader of this group was, without a doubt, a chemistry senior by the name of Paul Shiffer. Telling him seemed like the next steppingstone to leap to. Keep in mind that this was a tremendous step for a pathological loner. Terrified, I mustered the courage to walk down the hall and knock on his door.

The door opened and Paul greeted me, but with a somewhat puzzled look on his face, because we have never really spoken prior to this.

"I became a Christian a few nights ago, and I don't know what to do next." was my rehearsed opening line.

Paul became one of the most significant people in my life that day. He would become my first true friend. Someone who shaped my life, because his walk with God was genuine. He became my mentor and a lasting example of a life skillfully lived. He was engaged to a godly woman named Kathy. This would be one of the first functional families I would see and this also profoundly impacted my life. I wanted to be like Paul.

News of God's work in my life spread like wildfire within this campus ministry called The Navigators.[28] Christians seemed to come out of the woodwork and greeted me. I was invited to game nights, soccer games, Bible studies and other activities. The God Squad went to a Christian and Missionary Alliance Church every Sunday. They overloaded their cars beyond their seatbelt capacity, yet they made room for me. I met an entire parallel universe of people who knew God and walked with Him. I wanted the joy that these people had. I wanted the life that they lived, and I wanted their hope. Clearly, this was who

---

[28] A great campus and military Christian ministry

I was created to be. My eyes were opened to the Kingdom of God, and it was absolutely amazing.

For the first time in my life I belonged. For the first time in my life I could breathe. For the first time in my life I was alive. All this came about because I was forgiven. The key to this was trusting in the cross, not trusting in my deeds. Deeds are fig leaves; worthless when it comes to solving the problem of sin. I clipped into God's lifeline and was pulled from the tempest in the dead of night. Someone actually did notice my plight; someone did hear my Catskill prayer. The name of my rescuer is the very Son of God himself, Jesus, who actually rescued me 2000 years ago.

My efforts to be accepted by people by acting cool was nothing short of a dismal failure. Likewise, my efforts to earn God's favor by my good behavior was also clearly inadequate. I was a sinner, plain and simple, and hopelessly trapped. My fig leaves of performance that I followed without question, caused me to run from God and people. But like God seeking Adam in the garden, God sought after me in upstate New York, answering my prayer in the Catskills. He found me and held out a robe to cover my sin. Not garments of animal skins like he gave to Adam but a royal robe of righteousness.[29] A righteousness that is given to you, bought by the finished work of the cross, his perfect plan all along. Total forgiveness and an imputed righteousness was a gift presented to me. I had a choice: cling to my performance and credentials or cling to the cross. The correct choice was obvious.

Permanently adopted into God's family, completely forgiven, indwelled by His Spirit, baptized in Lake Ontario, I became a child of the Living God. Everything had changed in a single night; absolutely everything.

"Therefore, if anyone is in Christ, he is a new creation:
the old has gone, the new has come!"[30]

I am no longer who I was.

---

[29] Revelation 7:14, Zechariah 3:1-8

[30] 2 Corinthians 5:17

THE SOUP

In September of my sophomore year I returned to college as a new believer and, as luck would have it, the mother of all atheists landed on my dorm floor. He was insanely intelligent, had an encyclopedic memory, despised religion and held unswervingly to the position that if anyone believed the Bible, that person committed intellectual suicide. His room was across the hall from me, so avoidance of this abrasive person was difficult. He quickly picked up on the fact that he landed on the floor with the God Squad and he did not shy away from a debate. Time for some spiritual battle; let the games begin. His name was Steve. His French last name, unpronounceable by humans, was simply shortened to the phonetically similar first syllable of his surname; "Soup".

In our depraved state, sin effects people's minds differently, but everyone fundamentally misunderstands who God is and the means of restoring a relationship with Him is grossly misdirected. With Steve, he had a well-practiced intellectual objection which most Christians were woefully unprepared for. If you Googled "intellectual objection to the Bible", I am sure his photo would show up, if we had the internet back in 1980. How people are deceived varies from person to person but this was how sin affected the high-performance mind of The Soup.

After a few months of arguments, most of the God Squad lost interest and focused their attention on more receptive audiences. There simply was no convincing this guy of the Gospel. He was an enemy of God, unconvertible; I was the second to last to reach this conclusion.

Now when I say "argue" let me be clear that we were not quarreling or fighting. The polarized discussion was cordial, but there were clearly two sides and, at times, the points were quite blunt and direct. Neither one of us minded playing "hardball". Many times I had no answer for him and at times I lost the perspective that he was a captive in a prison camp and my role was to show him the unguarded hole in the wall. He actually brought up some good points from time to time but most of his objections fell into two categories. He was by no means a fan of the Catholic Church, where he was raised, and he didn't like Christians who were "brain dead", and he put them all into this category.

He did confess to me some time later that I did have one point that troubled him. It is known as Pascal's wager[31]. My version was:

"OK Steve, we are arguing over who is going to win in life, the Atheist or the Christian?"

"Correct." he replied.

"So, let's take case A, where, for the sake of argument, we will say that you, the Atheist are correct. There is no God and no Heaven or Hell. You live your life and I live my life. I am deceived, but other than that, there is substantially no difference in our lives, both of us say we have lived a good life."

A tentative "OK" from the Soup.

"Now, when we die there is, likewise, no difference between you and me. The same destiny awaits us both, whatever that might be, but we are in the same boat. You hold to the cease-to-exist model, so we both simply cease to exist."

"Yes, no major differences." the Soup cautiously concedes.

"Case B, I am correct. The Bible is true and there is a Heaven and Hell. You, the Atheist, live your life and I live mine. Ask either one of

---

[31] Google it

us while we are alive and neither would probably say we had any regrets over our choices. Same quality of life as in Case A, except in this case you are deceived."

"So, what is your point?" he jabbed.

"Well, when we die, we stand before the judgment seat of God, and I go to Heaven and you go to Hell."

"But the Bible is not true." the Soup quickly counters.

"Irrelevant! I submit that this is not a matter of the Bible being true or not; it is rather a matter of who cannot lose. Either case I cannot lose. You, on the other hand, are wagering eternity. You, absolutely, positively must be correct just to break even. I at a minimum, right now have that in the bag."

The Soup was finally silenced.

For a few moments he pondered the reality of this game. He lost sight of how high the stakes were but, to his credit, he is amongst the few that do seriously consider this eternal choice that is before all people. There are no spectators in this game. Every man, woman and child is "all in" on some position, and when the cards are laid down, there are no "do overs". Deciding to not decide, although a very popular option, is, in fact, a choice, and by no means a get-out-of-jail-free card.

He shared this with me about a year later during a conversation on the shores of Lake Ontario. Seven years later he would stand with me as my best man in my wedding. After many months of debate, he finally found the hole in the wall and escaped the prison that trapped him. He laid down his life at the cross and was born again. His powerful mind that argued against the faith was changed overnight and to this day remains a very powerful advocate and preacher of the truth found in the Bible. He has spent his life in professional ministry. He became my best friend.

Jesus Christ is in the life-changing business, and he intends to do so with every believer. This Gospel of grace is unstoppable and divinely powerful; it all starts with an invitation to "come and see".

The last person to write off the Soup as a lost cause was Paul Shiffer, the leader of the God Squad. Now a grad student in Chemistry, Paul was no slouch when it came to defending the faith. You cannot be brain dead and a grad student in chemistry at the same time, they are clearly mutually exclusive. Paul and I knocked on Soup's door one night with evangelical motives. Soup was an astronomy nut and physics major, so instead of having posters of scantily clad women he had astronomy posters. The most prominent one was of the Pleiades Cluster. Paul recognized this star group and identified it as we sat down. Steve was stunned that Paul knew this. Remember Steve thought all Christians did not have a brain. The Soup will now meet his match with Paul.

"You recognize the Pleiades cluster?"

"Yes, it is mentioned in the Bible you know."

"No way!" the Soup retorts.

"Yes, let me show you, as he turns to Job and flips through a few pages to find the obscure verse 38:31.

"Can you bind the beautiful Pleiades?[32]

The long and the short of that night was an assurance that there were sound reasons of evidence, history and philosophy that justify holding to the truthfulness of the Bible. Paul directly invited Steve to "come and see" by challenging him to read Josh McDowell's "Evidence that Demands a Verdict."[33] I squirmed a bit at this approach because this 400 page book is a tough read for most folks, but Steve accepted the challenge. We said we would be back in a week to discuss what he read. We handed him the book and departed.

Steve had the entire book read when we knocked on his door a week later. He was seriously wrestling with the idea that the Bible might be true. There was a web of lies that entangled Steve and his worldview was rapidly unraveling before his very eyes. I could see that his cage

---

[32] Please note that you have to be well read in the Scriptures to know this, Paul Shiffer epitomized this.

[33] A classic

was clearly rattled. Paul shared the Gospel message that night and I recall Steve physically reacting to the message. He literally got on his feet and ranted and raved about how simple the Gospel was and why was it that he never heard this before. This was a clear example of how the truth about grace and forgiveness trumps rumor theology. It's what I call "duh revelation", a sure sign of God speaking to someone.

We left him to contemplate this, and he later shared his head was spinning and that he lost sleep. The God Squad called in the heavy artillery and prayed anew for Steve. A few days later he was in the hall while the God Squad was informally hanging out in a room and the door was a few inches ajar. Nothing very spiritual was going on in the room but he eavesdropped on us for a minute or so and was compelled to reach one obvious conclusion: There was something different about these "born againers", and he longed to be one of them.

A day or two later the God Squad ambushed me in my room and said they had a surprise for me. I did not have a clue as to what this might be.

Paul came into the room and said, "Kurt I would like for you to meet your new brother in the Lord."

He opened the door and in stepped the Soup.

"For real?" I pressed Paul.

"Yes, he prayed to receive Jesus last night."

I stood up, met him in the middle of the room and with a very big smile extended my right hand and said, "Welcome to the Kingdom". We shook hands as brothers for the first time. This was the first conversion I was a part of and it was a whopper for sure. This Gospel works for lost causes like me, it is now clear that it works even for God's enemies, like Soup. The Gospel is indeed the greatest story of all and it is still going.

In the back of my mind though, a seed was planted. I was a sinner and so was the Soup. Neither one of us earned God's forgiveness. Neither one of us was what you would expect a Christian to be. Both of us fell horribly short of anything remotely resembling a decent life. However, the offer of forgiveness was real and we both jumped on it, no questions asked. But let it be known that it would take decades for that seed to grow. A fuller appreciation of what transpired, though not immediately apparent, would amaze me later in life as the bigger picture of the Gospel is revealed.

In my 40+ years of knowing Christ I have seen the Lord of Life redeem, reconcile and restore people from all sorts of dire straits. Victims and perpetrators, drug dealers and drug addicts, rich and poor, young and old, Satan worshipers and church goers, the cream of the crop and the scum of humanity all have been rescued and restored. Even the heroes of the Bible were deeply flawed. Moses was a murderer, King David an adulterer, Noah a drunk, the Apostle Paul a terrorist and the 12 disciples could just as easily been called the 12 stooges.

It is, without a doubt, that Jesus is in the life-changing business and this truth called "grace" is the horsepower driving this awesome message. The central message of the Bible is called the "Gospel". It's life-changing power is available to anyone. Anyone can be forgiven, no one is disqualified, it is offered to all.

But it is obvious that my early and simple understanding of the Gospel needed expansion. The "say the sinner's prayer, be good and get out of Hell Gospel" is wanting; good for salvation, but clearly incomplete. What are we dealing with here? What's really going on? There is an amazing life-altering power involved, more than a spiritual self-help program can explain. A complete lost cause like myself is restored. An enemy of God is completely reversed, something very powerful has been unleashed.

I felt I needed to put a handle on the bigger picture. The Gospel in America seems to have be reduced to a sales pitch for a prayer. I innately knew there was more, but comprehension eluded me for many years. I am, however, the type of person who asks the forbidden question, "What's in it for God?" A five-year-old kid provided this missing key dimension of the Gospel and moved me forward in my understanding.

But this is still merely a glimpse of what is going on in the big picture.

THE KID

Many years later, late at night, I find myself stopping at my usual grocery store to purchase a gallon of milk. Certainly not an unusual event, but an unexpected opportunity for God to show me an important point I was missing in my comprehension of the Gospel. I placed the car in park and noticed a young boy about five years old sitting by himself on a bench some distance from the store's entrance. Being a parent myself, I kept an eye on the kid from my car, hoping that a parent would present themselves so that I can get on with my task of acquiring milk. After several minutes, with no parent in sight, it is obvious that the kid was lost.

I hate these situations. I taught my kids that if they ever find themselves lost, they were to find a female employee and tell them that they need help. I know this is politically incorrect and no doubt profiling people, but I could care less about such nonsense. Safety for my kids was always paramount over hurting someone's feelings. Since I was the only one in the equation, responsibility to this kid fell to me, so away I went, as a male, to the rescue.

"Where are your parents?" I asked the youngster.

"I don't know."

"Do you mind if I just stay here with you until your parents find you?"

"Yeah."

So, I hung out with the kid. Now, small-town Montana in the 1990s was about as safe a place as you could find when it came to crime statistics. Loose cows were a common problem fielded by our sheriff's department, my kind of community. However, it was late at night, so I stood guard for the kid. No one would get any strange ideas when a 6 foot 4, Marine veteran was with him. Mom will be obvious when she arrives.

Still no mom after quite some time. Since the grocery store is the only nearby business still open, mom was probably there.

We walked into the grocery store and I found Anne, one of the managers. I don't know why, but between the pleasantries of cashier and customer, I concluded that she was a Christian woman, her faith seems obvious. She recognized me as a regular customer and I explained to her the dilemma of the lost child and how a PA system just might bring mother and child together. Her mothering instincts kicked in immediately and she took charge of the situation. The circumstance now in capable hands, I was back on mission to the dairy section as the PA system announced the found child.

By checkout time, mom still had not appeared, but I left knowing that the kid was in good hands. So out into the parking lot I went.

As I strolled to my car toting my prized gallon jug of 2%, it was glaringly obvious that mom was in the parking lot looking for her child. She had extended her search from the McDonalds across the street to the parking lot of the grocery store. She was going absolutely nuts as she frantically searched for her child. It was clear that she had dumped everything on her list of priorities except for a single point of focus. Her top and only item on her agenda was "Find child, whatever the cost".

"Looking for a lost boy?" I asked.

Never in my entire life, nor since, did I ever have anyone's instant and absolute full attention. "Yes! Yes!" was her desperate reply.

"In the grocery store with Anne, the manager." and then, without even a "Thank you", she was gone. Her lack of manners reflected her singular focus: Find child, whatever the cost.

"You will be like God.[34]" said the serpent. So, when we made self, the supreme being in our lives, we substituted faith in God for faith in self. Our relationship with our Heavenly Father, the ultimate parent, severed, we spiritually died. Mom in the parking lot revealed the heart of God; He went nuts[35]. He just lost His kids and absolutely nothing else mattered, save my kids whatever the cost.

What price needs to be paid to reverse the death of a child? The absolute ultimate agony of a parent is the death of their child. The English language fails to offer words that properly describe this. We, in turn, need to extend this perspective to our Heavenly Father in order to better understand the Gospel. The calamity of physical death exactly mirrors the cataclysmic consequences of spiritual death.

The clear-cut point is this; death destroys relationships, and the parent-child relationship is one of the deepest bonds we have, thus devastating when lost.

We deal with death many times in our lives and when we are confronted with the loss of a loved one, we ultimately contemplate in our minds that any price will be willingly paid to reverse the loss. Counselors call this stage of grief, "bargaining". It's as though somewhere in our soul we know that a price can be paid to undo the pain. Surely some sort of arrangement can be made but the details of

---

[34] Genesis 3:5

[35] My test readers had a lot of comments on "…He went nuts". To be clear this is not directly based on any Scripture it is my editorializing. I kept it just to get people to think. If there is celebration in Heaven when one sinner repents I expect that it would be a bad day when all of humanity crashed and burned.

the deal elude us. We eventually and painfully resign ourselves to the crushing permanence of death.

The plan for rescuing people from spiritual death starts to unfold in the Scriptures in Genesis chapter 3, blood must be shed. Blood symbolizes life in the Bible[36]. An exchange of life for death balances the ledger. My sin spiritually killed me, but I can be brought back to life. How? Take away my sin. Take away my sin means take away the death that cuts me off from my Father. The end game is stated in Colossians;

> *"but now He has reconciled you (to God) by Christ's physical body, through death to present you holy in his sight, without blemish and free from accusation"*[37].

Paul states, "This is the Gospel" in the very next sentence. This imputed or gifted righteousness that comes from the cross, not only takes away our sin, but, in fact also makes us holy. As a result, it brings us back to life and reconnects us to our Father, it is the very core message of the Bible. Spiritual death can, in fact, be completely reversed, but the cost is enormous and if you think you can foot this bill; think again.

Just like in Genesis 3, God must provide the solution, not us. This problem is not solved by what we "do" but rather by what Christ has "done". Reread the above verse from Colossians if you fail to grasp this, it's the cross that saves us, not what we do.

So, the mystery that solves spiritual death is revealed, it's called "The Gospel". It is paramount that our broken relationship with God be fixed, all other issues are secondary. However, this "free" Gospel is actually far from free. The tremendous cost to fix things was taken care

---

[36] Leviticus 17:11

[37] Colossians 1:21-22

of by the cross. The Father gave up everything near and dear to Him, His only Son. The Son emptied himself completely by laying down His life in a horrific death. The Father and Son foot the bill here, but the real kicker is it will cost you everything to embrace it. More on that in chapters to come, but for now, let's clearly establish that this seemingly unsolvable problem has indeed been solved. "It is finished"[38], were the last words of Jesus on the cross. This means the deal is done. Few grasp what has been done.

There is a fix, but there is a super important clause in this deal; it is offered to all, but only applies to those who receive Him. The Bible is quite clear on this point.

> *"Yet to all who received Him (Jesus), to those who believed in His name, He gave the right to become children of God. Children born not of natural descent, nor of human decision or a husband's will, but born of God."*[39]

Common sense dictates that only after you accept a gift can it be considered legally yours and so it is with the Gospel, you have to accept it. This crucial first step is often missed by many. This necessary response was mind blowing for me when I was first told of it, but it is still only a partial understanding of what the substance of the Gospel is truly about. A lesson in the Philippines further clarifies the big picture that a person's acceptance of the cross is only the beginning, but that is the next chapter...

The hole in the bottom of the boat has been busted wide opened. We can now swim to the realm that we were created for; a Spirit-to-spirit unity with the Almighty God where Jesus is Lord, Savior and Teacher. The diagnostic question is simple, is that where you want to be?

---

[38] John 19:30

[39] John 1:12-13

Enter Uzzah

A cool difference between the Old and New Testaments is that in the New Testament Jesus uses everyday experiences to teach spiritual principles via parables. However, in the Old Testament, the mechanism tends to be more history and symbolism. So, when the Old Testament is studied, we run across the strange story of Uzzah[40] and we are initially baffled by this obscure and odd anecdote of history until we understand how its core lesson reverberates through the remainder of the Scriptures.

So, to set the stage of Uzzah, the Israelites needed to move the ark of the covenant (Yes, Raiders of the Lost Ark). They screwed this up by using an ox cart instead of the special poles God required for just such an occasion. The seemingly well-intentioned endeavor starts out on the wrong foot. The narrative then tells us that during the move, the oxen stumbled and Uzzah steadied the ark so as to prevent it from falling off the cart. God zapped him on the spot. Whoa! cut the guy some slack. What was he supposed to do? But we must understand that the ark represented the very presence of God. Nobody, absolutely nobody comes into the presence of God without dealing with the problem of sin. A Holy God does not tolerate sin. Good intentions by people are a step in the right direction, but fall far short of solving the issue of sin, this is non-negotiable.

The veil.

Now another seemingly unrelated detail concerns the veil of the temple. This thick curtain separates a room known as the "Holy of Holies" from the rest of the Temple. The ark of the covenant is in this room,[41] there is only one way into this room and it is blocked by the veil. Do not enter is the message here.

Levitical Law dictates that once a year, the High Priest would have to go into the Holy of Holies and sprinkle the blood of a special sacrifice

---

[40] 2 Samuel 6:6

[41] Exodus 26:33

on the ark. This is The Day of Atonement or better known as Yom Kippur.[42] Thanks to Uzzah, the High Priest had a measurable level of trepidation about this task. One false move and like Uzzah, zap! The priest would be dead. That left the attending staff arguing over who would go in and retrieve the body. There were no volunteers, again thanks to Uzzah.

So, someone with forward thinking skills came up with a solution; tie a rope around the ankle of the High Priest. If he got zapped in the Holy of Holies, the attendants could pull his body from the room without entering it. Thus, no collateral zaps. The High Priest was on his own but at least the staff was safe. The rope showed how seriously they took this. It was extremely clear in their minds; God will not tolerate sin. There are no excuses and no exceptions. The Jewish High Priests understood this and proceeded with the most extreme of caution, and fear thanks to Uzzah.[43]

Sin, and the resulting spiritual death, is clearly the uncrossable barrier that separates us from God. The veil symbolizes this absolute. Unfortunately, this simple truth is often misrepresented by religious jabbering and pontification that distracts us from the obvious point. The fundamental prerequisite for any relationship is straight forward; both parties must be alive. You cannot have a relationship with a dead person, there must be life. God is alive, we are dead, this doesn't work. The veil paints the picture of this reality; although we are biologically alive, we are spiritually dead, and consequently, our relationship with God is destroyed.

The Apostle Paul lays out a before and after that matches the before and after represented by the Old and New Testaments; the before…

> *"As for you, you were dead in your transgressions and sins, in which you used to live when you followed the*

---

[42] Leviticus 16

[43] This is a debated point of history and certainly not found in the Bible but never the less, very conceivable

ways of this world .... Like the rest, we were by nature deserving of wrath."[44]

The layout of the Temple clearly shows us that we cannot enter the presence of God on our own, we are cut off. Access to God is impossible, but before we get sucked into the hopelessness of the situation, let's remember two important facts about the Temple; the High Priest can cross and fix things and veils are temporary not permanent. This is what the Day of Atonement symbolizes. However, for the High Priest to do this, a life (blood) must be offered to bring the dead back to life.

The New Testament records that Jesus did exactly that, via the cross. Not just temporarily and symbolically but rather the permanent and final resolution of this problem.[45] The Perfect High Priest offered the Perfect Sacrifice that is the Perfect Solution to make people perfect. The veil of the Temple was not just gently pushed aside, it was destroyed at the moment of the Messiah's death, ripped apart from top to bottom.[46] This event represents a tectonic shift in the fabric of the spiritual world. The problem of spiritual death was shredded by Calvary.

The garden variety Joe can now be made spiritually alive and can have his relationship with his Heavenly Father restored. The Spirit is no longer sparingly doled out to special folks on a temporary or limited basis, as in the Old Testament. Pentecost demonstrate a huge change in the New Testament; the Spirit and life is now poured out, on a wholesale basis, to everyone that embraces the cross. God is no longer afar, the spiritually dead can be reborn and brought to life. A relationship with our Father is now a real possibility. This new life is in His Son[47]. Paul concludes his before and after the cross lesson:

---

[44] Ephesians 2:1-3

[45] Hebrews 9:26-28

[46] Matthew 27:51

[47] 1 John 5:11-12

"But because of his great love for us, God, who is rich in mercy, made us alive with Christ even when we were dead in transgressions—it is by grace you have been saved."[48]

God provided the ultimate and only solution; a path of rebirth and new life. A hole has been punched through the bottom of the boat. The fish torn from the relational ocean from which it was created for, can swim to it's natural realm and not only live, but now thrive in a Spirit to spirit unity with the Almighty God. Self-supremacy, however, must be exchanged for the supremacy of Christ in order to reconnect with the Father. Everything can be forgiven. The cataclysmic consequences of sin can be undone. A person's sin can be exchanged for the righteousness of Christ. Spiritual death can be exchanged for spiritual life. All by the finished work of the cross, all by God's grace, all by His unconditional love for us, all because He went nuts because his kids were lost.

We lose sight of this and think that the Bible is God stapling up "lost cat" posters on telephone poles in His neighborhood, but, in fact His singular focus is "Find child, whatever the cost." We are made in His image, we are His children, we are not His pets. His love for us is demonstrated by the cost he paid, His only Son. I will die for my kids, but when the vet bill starts pushing $500, sorry cat. Yes, we are that valuable. The universal currency of value is sacrifice. What did God sacrifice to save me? I am shattered by the cost of my sin and I am stunned by my value to God.

The cosmic power play of the cross starts to make sense in light of the mother and child reunion. The rigid wall surrounding my simplistic understanding of the Gospel starts to crack. I can feel it in my bones, there is still so much more to this Gospel, but what am I missing, more pieces of the puzzle elude me.

But for now, some key points are obvious; this is not a do-it-yourself religion. I did not fix this; Jesus did. He broke through the wall of death; not me. More importantly, I didn't do anything to earn this in

---

[48] Ephesians 2:4-5

fact I screwed everything up in the first place to land myself in this predicament. The hero here is Jesus!

> *"but it has now been revealed through the appearing of our Savior, Christ Jesus, who has destroyed death and has brought life and immortality to light through the gospel."*[49]

The big picture starts to unfold. This rescue is of paramount importance to the Father and the only reason for this is because of His parental love for us. The mechanism of rescue is grace and forgiveness. It, likewise, should be absolutely first and foremost in our life's priorities as well. Nothing else matters until this is settled.

> *"For God so loved the world that he gave his one and only Son, that whoever believes in him shall not perish but have eternal life."*[50]

The focal point of history and the entire creation centers on the Father rescuing His kids. Find child, whatever the cost.

---

[49] 2 Timothy 1:10

[50] John 3:16

THE ESCAPE

The flight deck of the USS Pelilieu[51] was some 90 feet above the harbor's water of Subic Bay Naval Base in the Philippines, so it offered a decent vantage point of the adjacent town of Olongapo. As we approached the dock, from what I could see, Olongapo was stuck in the quagmire of abject poverty. The prevailing architectural style was third world ghetto, the likes of which middle class Americans, like myself, are sheltered from and thus have difficulty comprehending. There was a strip of neon and modern buildings extending from the main gate of the base, down Main Street, perhaps a half mile long at best. Downtown Olongapo was the home of 25 cent San Miguel beer and an abundance of working women, who would provide their services for as little as five dollars back in 1985. If their English was sketchy, they simply groped you on the street with a smile. This was not the moral capital of the world, and certainly not the destination of choice for a Christian man, but there I stood on the flight deck, pondering this spectacle as the ship got tied up.

---

[51] USS Peliieu LHA (Landing ship Helicopter Assault) is basically an aircraft carrier for helicopters

Shore leave for 72 hours. After many weeks at sea, a cold beer and a decent steak at the Officer's Club was pretty high on my "to do" list. I would also enjoy being in a world, for a few days, that had color other than gray or green. I stood on the flight deck as we arrived. Three days later when we departed, I would stand in the exact same spot, but with my understanding of the Gospel significantly adjusted.

As with many who visit a third world country, we are often jolted from our perspective of things, especially after meeting someone face to face. After a few beers with the boys on our first day, I would make my way back to my stateroom[52] onboard the ship and sleep comfortably in my rack. The woman I would meet the next day was most likely going to sleep hungry or would share a bed with a stranger, paid for her services.

The stage was set for the perfect storm that would bring me into a deeper understanding of the Gospel. I stumbled through rather unexpected circumstances that bordered on the bizarre. The lesson would not be about a simple fix but rather, transplanting someone from one world to another, so a new life can be categorically overhauled.

Believe it or not, to set the stage for our theological lesson, I must first, pass on some details about the local bar girls[53]. This information is standard fare in a liberty brief prior to docking in a Philippine port. Sit down at a table in a club and a young girl will be sitting on your lap in less than a minute. A gentle "no thanks" and another takes her place, you can't win so you just go with it. At this point she is just "eye candy" and a companion. She works for the bar and her job is to get you to buy her a watered down and overpriced drink. Paid by the drink, her take home for the night might be $2. Now if someone is so inclined to take the arrangement to the next level, one would have to pay the bar owner a "bar fine" ($10) and she is released from her shift and allowed

---

[52] Stateroom sounds cool but it was basically a walk in closet that housed 4 junior officers.

[53] "Bar girls" were at the top of the working women status, "street walkers" the lowest

to leave. Arranging additional services for the evening can then be negotiated with her separately. Most of these girls hover in the 15-18 year old demographic, heartbreaking to say the least.

To say that I am not a party person is a gross understatement; in fact, I genuinely dread them. People are wired differently. Loud music, dancing and general craziness has no appeal to me at all. I must be missing this gene. Parties are a social event, yet this is where I feel most alone. To most people, this is incomprehensible, being alone in a room full of people. It seems to be an oxymoron, but to others they know exactly what I am describing. Nevertheless, one of the customs amongst Marine Corps Officers is the all too frequent "officer's call", aka a party. Stateside these tended to be a BBQ at the Executive Officer's house or a round of beer at the Officer's Club on a Friday afternoon, but "when in Rome"...our battalion reserved an entire nightclub for the event. As per usual, attendance by all officers was expected.

So, the next evening I find myself sharing a table with some fellow lieutenants at a Philippine night club. Music was blaring, drinks flowed and a pretty local gal sitting on my lap, smiling and in Pidgin English, "You buy me drink?". I bought the drink and struggled through some small talk with her, fighting loud music and broken English. I enjoyed this as much as getting my fingernails pulled out. Again, far from my normal hangout...but it was, at a minimum, a change of pace from the humdrum of shipboard life.

From time to time the club owner, who acted as the emcee for the evening, would grab a mike and blurb something from the dance floor. I basically ignored this nonsense, waiting for the end of this tiresome ordeal, so I could go back to the ship. My ear caught a key detail, "The final event for the evening..." it appeared to be a raffle for some gag door prizes.

"And the grand prize winner is...Lieutenant Blomback"

"Blombo[54] you won!"

"What?!"

"Blombo you won, go get your prize"

I went up and got my prize, which was a coupon for a bar girl's "bar fine". Now just to be clear, the club raffled off a working woman and the Christian won. Most likely a set up, I was caught flat footed and speechless. I took the coupon from the man. The irony of the situation was obvious to several of my fellow officers, they raised their drinks and cheered loudly. I returned to my chair, folded the coupon and stuffed it in my pocket, this would never be used.

However, the flashing neon lights of the stage were like the silent flashes of lightning from a distant storm. It's eye and me, were set to collide, knocking me from my comfort zone and into the heartache of a person trapped in the third world. My lesson for a deeper understanding of the Gospel awaited, my teacher was a Filipino woman, working the oldest profession, whom I just won in a raffle. This is hardly the setting one would expect for a lesson in theology but the class; Escape 101 was now in session.

The formalities of the evening concluded, the party continued, I tarried a bit. This 16-year-old girl has been sitting on my lap for almost two hours now and she asked me to dance. Most Marines are quite adept at combat skills, capable of killing an enemy in seconds with their bare hands, but few of them dance even remotely close to the benchmark of "cool". It seems to be a mutually exclusive skill set. I was no exception to this rule; moreover, I would put dancing close to the bottom of the list of my talents, just above floral arrangements. A quick look at fellow officers slow dancing with their partners, a simple swaying back and forth to the music. I could fake that, or so I thought, so against my better judgment, I said "yes" to her dance request.

Yup, I screwed it up (alcohol a factor), I did not do the math. The spectacle was rather comical, as I am 6'4", in the 99th percentile for physical height. Filipinos are significantly shorter than Americans,

---

[54] "Blombo" was my Marine nickname, a combination of Blomback and Rambo

their women even more so. This gal was five foot nothing. This was obviously not working, so I picked her up and placed her on an empty pedestal that the stage dancers used, problem solved. She could now rest her chin on my shoulder instead of my belt buckle. The next song was by the group Foreigner. She knew the words of this classic 80's song by heart and sung it softly and sadly in my now accessible ear.

"I want to know what love is

I want you to show me

I wanna feel what love is

I know you can show me"

At first, I thought it was a "come on", based on her profession, but something in her voice reflected a deep sense of lost, hopelessness and pain of being an unlovable bar girl. Any hope for a healthy relationship was traded in a long time ago for survival. She was crushed by poverty, trapped and caught in an unthinkable end game. The sudden realization that this young girl was derailed by poverty and forced into a life of shame shocked me out of my comfort zone. This was absolutely no place for a 16-year-old child! I held the ticket for her escape, at least for tonight, in my pocket. I did what I never ever expected to do, I paid her bar fine with my coupon, then escorted her out. Please note, my intentions were honorable; I would treat her like a lady for one night, with dinner and conversation.

After two hours, it was getting late and it was time to say, "Goodbye, nice meeting you." She offered an opportunity for additional services, which I declined, but paid her anyhow. Pocket change for me was a month's wage for her. I continued with the "Goodbyes". She, however, was very insistent that I see her tomorrow, "off the clock". I caved in and agreed, reasoning that I could use a guide as I shopped for local goods to send back home. We set a lunch date and spent the afternoon shopping. I spent about another month of her wages on her that afternoon. She had to go to the bar to start her work and I must return to my ship because it leaves at noon tomorrow. Again "goodbyes" failed against her, "please, please, please!" and I get suckered into an early breakfast date.

After breakfast, I absolutely positively must say, “goodbye”. My ship was scheduled to leave in a few hours and the Marines, for some reason, got really upset if you missed the boat. It was then that I found myself on the receiving end of a desperate and tearful embrace. What was going on here? She wanted to marry me! “What! Are you nuts?” I really had to go, as I pried her from myself. She then jumped on me and wrapped both her arms and legs around me, and then, semi hysterically, with copious tears flowing, again, begged me to marry her! “Please, please, please!” with desperation and promises of all kinds. The situation spiraled wildly out of control as she repeatedly kissed me. This girl has gone completely psycho on me. I was genuinely taken aback by this spectacle. I had difficulty getting the time of day from women back in the States and here this gal was begging me to marry her in less than 36 hours! I absolutely must leave NOW, she will not take “no” for an answer. I ultimately broke her heart and departed.

I walked up to the main gate of Subic Naval Base, the motif of fences, barbed wire, warning signs and Military Police clearly communicated the message of “authorized personnel only”. High and tight, lean and mean, the guards silently cast a quick glance at my military ID, a formality at best. As someone “in the Marine Corps”, I casually stepped from one world into another, leaving her behind.

Desperately trying to put a handle on my experience, I flaunted my relational illiteracy to a fellow officer as I shared the story of this gal. Confused, I ask him what his take on things were. His reply was straight forward:

“Kurt, you are the only person who has ever treated her like a human being. You were kind to her. If she marries you, she escapes this hell hole of poverty and goes to a new life in America. She would be a fool not to take her chances with you”.

I viewed her as a pleasant distraction, but she saw me as her escape from one life and a ticket to a new life in the United States, just an “I do” away. She went “all in” on me. Wow, I just pegged a 1.2 out of 10 on the clueless meter!

We prepared for departure with headcounts and all sorts of stuff like that. Then, I made my way back up to the fan tail of the flight deck. The ways of tugboats and deck hands have always been curiously entertaining to me. So, I stood in the exact same spot as before, as the ship readied itself for departure. The ship departed and the waters of Subic Bay were churning below me. I was among the few that remained on the flight deck.

Being a reflective person, the parallels to the Gospel message were now clear. There was a vast and hopelessly uncrossable barrier between my Filipino friend and the life that she wanted to live in the US. Even if she could cross, she would still have lacked a legitimate legal status. Her solution of marriage was a bold move and, although born out of desperation, it was quite genius. If she entered a covenant relationship with me, both problems would be solved; as my rights and resources as a US citizen became hers as well. She would get the legal status as a citizen, and I would then fly her to the States. United with me in marriage, she would be dead to her old life, some 7000 miles of ocean away, and henceforth treated like a lady. She didn't want to go to the US to work the streets, she wanted to live a new life of dignity. Her begging for marriage were cries for help to escape her world. "Marry me" was in fact, best translated as, "save me".

I would like to revisit the pre-eminent condition of my life in my early unsaved days; rejection. This phase in my life, although painful, actually produced a beneficial outcome in my life. It made me very sensitive to an essential but intangible attribute of relationships, that is, the dimension of formal inclusion and belonging, and from this vantage, Scriptures that mention "in Christ" leap from the page with great clarity. My short time with my new Filipino friend brought this obvious, but often overlooked, truth to a higher level of comprehension.

Many promises of God fall into the "conditional" category, to wit: a condition must be met in order for the promise to apply or be true for a person. Let's get your attention by example and then explain.

"Therefore, there is now no condemnation for those who are in Christ Jesus"[55]

"In Him we have redemption through His blood, the forgiveness of sins"[56]

But now in Christ Jesus you who once were far away have been brought near through the blood of Christ"[57]

There are dozens of such promises found in the New Testament. Virtually all implicitly or explicitly state the condition that must be met in order for the promise to be true; that person must be "in Christ". This non-negotiable, must have, point of belonging is keenly understood by folks like myself who don't seem to belong and whose default setting is rejection. We have this raw nerve exposed; we get this.

Rumor theology concedes a bell curve distribution of moral performance (works righteousness), Mother Teresa on one end, Hitler on the other, and most of us somewhere in the middle. There are several errors that most people hold to concerning God's promises and the bell curve.

These promises apply to everybody on the curve

These promises only apply to the good half

These promises only apply to those who believe them

It does not even take any real attention to the text, to show that all these are completely wrong, since the condition is very clearly stated in the Scriptures to the point of nauseous repetition. Everything rides on being "in Christ".

---

[55] Romans 8:1

[56] Ephesians 1:7

[57] Ephesian 2:13

So, what does it mean to be “in Christ”? Well, it does not get any clearer than Romans 8:9:

> *“If anyone does not have the Spirit of Christ, he does not belong to Christ.”*

Yes, there is a bell curve distribution of performance, but the Bible is abundantly clear in that this is irrelevant. There are only two groups of people; those “in Christ” and those that are not. Those that have the Spirit and those that do not.

The “in Christ” crowd enjoy a formal covenant relationship with Christ, His rights and resources are mine as well. This deal has been sealed by His Spirit at the moment of belief as per Ephesians 1:13-14:

> *"And you also were included in Christ when you heard the word of truth, the gospel of your salvation. Having believed you were marked in him with a seal, the promised Holy Spirit, who is a deposit guaranteeing our inheritance"*

Now, it is somewhat common to refer to a “covenant” as a “contract”. Business contracts are a binding agreement by two parties. Generally, it specifies actions of trust and selflessness in order to attain a greater good for both parties. This, of course, is the most common understanding of “covenant”, but this cold legal definition is not even close to what the Bible describes. The higher understanding of “covenant” is better understood as an agreement to combine lives via selfless love. Marriage is the obvious example here, not a 50/50 business deal, but rather the combining or unity of two people. “They will become one flesh” as the author of Genesis writes[58]. Self-importance and unity are very much inversely proportional. Like the playground seesaw, both “individuals” have to descend in the self-important department, in order to raise up a new “us”.

The result is that all resources and privileges are now shared when lives are combined. In my marriage it is “our house”, “our money”, “our

---

[58] Genesis 2:24

kids". Yes, we have a "mom's car" and a "dad's car" but that simply semantically clarifies who primarily drives one of "our cars".

Likewise, Christians are the "Bride of Christ",[59] combined lives, where we share in His righteousness, His inheritance, His privileges and rights as God's child, and we have full access to the Father "In His name".[60] We are, in fact, as righteous as Jesus, as we also share his righteousness,[61] It's been given to us. We ultimately share His indestructible life which we call "eternal life". This covenant is the highest of all covenants and requires on our part, what Romans 12 calls a "living sacrifice"[62].

The formal uniting of my life with His, is the New Covenant or New Testament ushered in, authored and perfected by Jesus and sealed with His blood. It is in fact, a sacred blood oath, rock solid and irreversible. It really is the instantaneous legal restoration of our originally created status as a member of God's family (justification). The powerhouse of the Trinity, the indwelling Holy Spirit, seals the deal, then starts the process of restoring the quality of our relationship to the Father (sanctification). But it all starts with accepting the proposal of marriage; all the rights and resources of the very Son of God can indeed be mine. But first things first; Jesus must take His rightful place in our lives as Lord, Savior and Teacher.[63] Self must step down from the throne. Again note, the seesaw arrangement.

We can escape the prison of self by dying to self and remaking Christ supreme via the cross. When we choose this, we find great joy in restoring our original relationship with God, i.e. being Christ's slave.

---

[59] Ephesians 5:22-33

[60] John 15:16

[61] 2 Corinthians 5:21

[62] Romans 12:1

[63] Receiving Jesus as Lord, Savior and Teacher is implicit in conversion, but deliberately addressing each of these issues after conversion clarifies the role that Jesus plays in our lives going forward

This obviously counterintuitive point of truth may take decades to appreciate, but the Apostle Paul, the best teacher of grace, constantly refers to himself as Christ's slave, bondservant or servant.[64] This reflects his deep understanding of selflessness.

> *"I have been crucified with Christ and I no longer live, but Christ lives in me. The life I live in the body, I live by faith in the Son of God, who loved me and gave himself for me"*[65]

Our sin nature recoils at such words but also appreciate that the New Testament uses descriptors such as "friend", "child", "brother", "ambassador" and "royal priesthood" to describe our new position of freedom in Him. There is a lot to absorb here, with massive ramifications, I will simply refer you to Neil Anderson's "Victory Over Darkness, The Power of Your Identity in Christ" for an immersive study of this topic. I take great comfort in the benevolence and grace of God. After 40+ years, I will never go back, and I take great comfort in identifying myself as "a servant of the Risen Christ". In light of his grace and our created purpose, the totality of my being remains the only appropriate response, a joining of two lives, a covenant relationship, the whispered secret for slipping from the prison of self, a far cry from the "say a prayer.... get out of Hell" Gospel.

So, let's step back and look at some big picture stuff. Salvation is not by a thing, not a lifeboat, not a rope, not a secret password and certainly not by what we do. Rescue is by a person and that person is not you. We are saved by the actions of someone else. This rescuer is Jesus. His life, death and resurrection is what saves people. Our connection to Him is paramount, we must be family.

---

[64] 1 Peter 2:16, Romans 1:1

[65] Galatians 2:20

"How great is love the Father has lavished on us, that we should be called children of God! And that is what we are."[66]

I watched Olongapo slip into the horizon, my heart was genuinely grieved by her circumstance. Soon nothing but ocean was visible. Heading East across a vast ocean, the USS Peleliu turned her screws and headed towards California, our time overseas was done, it was time to go home.

A few weeks later, California appeared on the horizon, we manned the rails of the ship as is the custom when a naval ship arrives in a harbor. As we steamed into the harbor at Long Beach, California, Neil Diamond's "Coming to America" blared over the ship's 1MC system. This was perhaps the most patriotic moment of my life. When I stepped off the ship onto the dock, I am a citizen, this is my home. When I get to heaven, I will belong there also; not just because I am just a citizen, but more importantly because I am family. I am finally going to see my Father eyeball to eyeball. Saved by God's grace in March of 1980, the uncrossable barrier of sin solved by the cross, I became a member of the church, Christ's bride[67], and entered an irreversible covenant relationship with the risen Christ, a child of God. I have escaped the kingdom of darkness and have stepped into a new life in the Kingdom of God. The Gospel is not a contest of performance…. It is a covenant of unity.

The grandest of all celebrations will be given on the day of the resurrection; the wedding supper of the lamb[68], it will be the mother of all welcome home parties. I think it will be the first party I will actually enjoy.

---

[66] 1 John 3:1

[67] Revelation 19:7

[68] Revelation 19:9 The wedding supper of the Lamb

Feeling like I knew nothing; God lead me back to faith. I have been walking with God by faith for years. I got this, or so I thought. The entirety of the Gospel rides on this single word: faith. As such, the term is recklessly thrown around in the church these days way too often. So, a revisit of this essential word was warranted. I spit blood, dirt and grass as my next lesson from The Teacher clobbered me.

THE PARACHUTE

"Wake up! You have to wake up NOW!" I screamed to myself as I execute my all too familiar routine of emerging from unconsciousness. As a general rule, when you are unconscious things have gone terribly wrong. Restoring soundness of mind and situational awareness is the first order of business. Thoughts are random at this point and the brain struggles to sort them by importance and sequence, and, to my alarm, the early facts cause me to utter an expletive. I was emerging from unconsciousness after I had parachuted out of an airplane at night. There is no way that this can be good. Details were sketchy, but signs of hope appeared. My face was in the dirt and a considerable amount of grass was uncomfortably lodged in my mouth. Next, I wiggled my toes and fingers to check for a spinal injury. So far so good. A parachuting accident of some sort but I am on the ground without debilitating spinal injuries, I am cleared to move, and I struggled to my feet.

"Oh no! Someone else is hurt." I thought as the remembrance of events streamed clearer through my prefrontal cortex. I was in Fort

Benning, Georgia at Army Airborne School,[69] standing in the pitch dark of some remote drop zone, the faint images of fellow jumpers gathering their chutes and the roar of a C-141 aircraft overhead as another string of jumpers, barely visible, popped out of the rear of the plane.

A few blinks to refocus my eyes and now I recalled that when I jumped from the plane, my chute appeared to be wrapped around my head. Our instructor told us, with excellent deadpan delivery, not to worry about such things, "You have the rest of your life to take corrective action...probably up to 12 seconds."

I pulled the chute from my face and balled it up, because one must make the dreaded cut loose and deploy the reserve chute decision during such a crisis since a shredded main chute can tangle up the reserve chute. If that happened, then you have a real problem, since there was no plan "C" other than survive the thud; which by the way, was not generally endorsed by our instructors.

I checked my main chute, but wait, it looked good. I double, then triple checked everything, all was good. The poor sap that jumped ahead of me must be in a world of hurt. I figured his chute must have gotten shredded and wrapped around my face, and he was taking the express lane to Mother Earth. I stuffed the remnants of the chute into my uniform shirt; there are no time outs in this game. I had a landing to execute, somewhere in the dark, the ground was coming up fast.

Now as the clarity of events progresses from alarming to humorous. Bear in mind the darkness of Georgia nights and the adrenaline rush of jumping out of an airplane with full combat gear, at night, 1250 feet above the hard ground. The parachute that I pulled from my face was actually my own poncho. It got ripped out from the outer pocket of my pack during the "Maytag moment" where I was tossed around like a rag doll as I exited a perfectly good airplane traveling at 130 mph. No one was hurt after all, except me. The question remained; how did I get clocked?

---

[69] The US Marine Corps uses many US Army schools

Our fifth and final jump of the school was this night jump with full combat gear. Our packs hung in front of our knees and were clipped to a quick-release pins around your waist and tethered by a 30-foot strap. Our reserve chute covered our stomachs, and our main chute was on our backs. Add a rifle in a case and one could barely move. As you waddled like a penguin to the exit door, in the dim red-light interior, the scene approached comical. The jumpers ahead of you turned into a blur as they exited the plane and were swept away by the airstream.

We were told that we should release our packs 100 feet above the ground and let it dangle from the 30-foot strap. This provided some freedom of movement so we could execute our often practiced Parachute Landing Fall (PLF) and avoid injury.

All this sounded nice during ground training, but the reality of the situation was that this moonless night in Georgia was so dark that judging altitude was impossible. My best guess was that I was passing 300 feet and I saw no harm in dangling my pack early. So, I popped the release pins and felt the pack hit the end of the strap, and then, in an instant, it went slack. I wondered how my strap could have broken, because it was strong enough to lift a horse. Then I woke up on the ground with a poncho in my shirt and spitting grass, blood and dirt from my mouth.

Unbeknownst to me, I released my pack at 50 feet instead of 300. The slack was not the strap breaking at all, but rather, it was the pack hitting the ground. Clueless and blind because of the dark and descending faster because of the added weight, the ground hit me like a freight train. Cold cocked and just shy of a concussion, I gathered my gear and stumbled to the rally point. Just another day at the office for a Recon Marine.

So, what does jumping out of an airplane have to do with the Bible? It is an excellent opportunity to clarify a definition. Insert a wrong definition into a Biblical command and a lie is given birth. It sounds right, but something is fishy. It's called rumor theology, and it is everywhere. So, let's look into the definition of the frequently used word "faith".

It's never a question of having faith or not, it is rather a question of the object of your faith. Christians have learned the buzz phrase “saved by faith” but insert a wrong object of faith in that statement via mis definition and you can get a serious fig leaf. It sounds correct, but it is fundamentally flawed. This error will absolutely go undetected if the object (the cross) is not specifically stated. If it is vague and implied, things usually go very wrong.

Let us examine three very common mis-definitions of “faith” and then we will look at the Biblical definition of “faith”. Finally, we will diagnose who really is the person you have put your faith in.

But before we dive into this, let's get scholarly for a moment and acknowledge that the phrase “saved by faith” does indeed appear in the Church these days, but we must also recognize that this is an often-shortened phrase which is more precisely stated as “For it is by grace you have been saved, through faith.”[70] To be clear, the life, death and resurrection of God's Son is what saves us; our response to this tremendous act of love (grace) is faith. The object of our faith, Jesus, is the key point here. So, let's keep this in mind as we proceed.

The first mis-definition of faith we have to address is the one where one's religious lifestyle is considered “faith”. Virtually any spiritualized, ethereal mindset can be considered “faith” these days. Always speak on a higher plane of enlightenment with religious gibberish generously thrown in and one can elicit the “oohs” and “aahs” of their listeners. Winston Churchill said it best, “if you can't convince them, confuse them”. Spiritualized buzz words create the word salad that impresses or confuses ordinary people. All sorts of nonsense gets passed off as legit, false religions, as well as fortune cookie and bumper sticker theology, to name a few.

The masses swayed, self also becomes swayed and the self-deception inherent with pride lulls the victim into a false sense of security. Nothing could be further from the truth. Do you trust in Christ, or do you trust in your “faith”? This is a faith in Christ or faith in faith

---

[70] Ephesians 2:8

issue. The latter of course is a spiritualized form of faith in self, the root of all fig leaves. Obviously, this is a "no-go", but going forward, listen closely and read between the lines and you will see how many people buy into this nonsense.

So, the second mis-definition of faith is the all-too-common meaning that faith is a matter of blind wishful thinking; a resolute conclusion that is not based on any evidence. The close cousin of this is the idea that something becomes true because I believe it. This is super common, but completely wrong and the parachute brings this to light. You see the parachute clearly does not work because of my hope. The chute does not deploy because of my belief in its existence. The harness does not hold me because I have spoken a faith utterance. Name it and claim it has nothing to do with it either. The gear works independently of what I think, say and do. I leap out of the plane in <u>response</u> to knowing that the gear is ridiculously trustworthy. I trust and rely on the gear, so I leap into the void.

To further our understanding of the inherent flaw of this second mis-definition, we have to go back to how the Army's Airborne School was set up to. Before we jumped, we went through a full week of classes and drills to learn technique and to build our trust in our gear. You see the Army has figured out, that people not trusting the gear leads to what is called a "weak exit". This is where someone hesitates as they jump out of the plane. This is where the vast majority of mishaps occur, the jump must be clean. A half jump opens up the possibilities of so many things going wrong and is ultimately rooted in people not trusting the gear and the technique. The trustworthiness of both must be absolute and it is learned on the ground it in a variety of simulations during the first week of the two week school.

This brainless mis-definitions of "faith" is completely non-Biblical and derails so many of its adherents and is a major turn off to many seekers who value critical thinking. That is why I propose doing away with the word "faith" entirely and replacing it with the word "trust". The "trust" in the Bible is entirely based on clear and convincing evidence and our response to it. This trust or reliance is identical to the trust and reliance a parachutist has in the gear that will safely get him to the ground.

Biblical trust and reliance in the cross gets oneself safely through the pearly gates of heaven.

Note how Jesus appealed to evidence when he answered John the Baptist followers. This is the faith, trust and reliance that the Bible speaks of.

> *"Jesus replied, "Go back and report to John what you hear and see: The blind receive sight, the lame walk, those who have leprosy are cured, the deaf hear, the dead are raised, and the good news is preached to the poor."*[71]

The exhortation by Jesus is clear; use your brain to trust the obvious conclusion based on the evidence that is clearly seen and heard; He is the Messiah.

Look at the entire Book of John in the New Testament. It is a record of the clear and convincing evidence surrounding the life of Jesus. There is no sales pitch here by John to shut off your brain; in fact, he compels his readers to rather engage their brain. The teaching, miracles and resurrection are clearly expounded in his eyewitness account. There is no one even remotely in the same category as Jesus. It is clear to any thinking person, that Jesus is the Messiah.

John is a masterpiece of evidence, and it should be noted that the following verse appears right after "Doubting Thomas" demands evidence, which, by the way, he gets.

> *"Jesus did many other miraculous signs in the presence of his disciples, which are not recorded in this book. But these are written that you may believe that Jesus is the Christ, the Son of God, and that by believing you may have life in his name."*[72]

Nowhere in the New Testament is "faith" defined as mindless wishful thinking. And for the record, you are not saved by the sincerity of your

---

[71] Matthew 11:4

[72] John 20:30

faith either. It is always a question of the object of your faith. A mustard seed of trust in the cross trumps a bucket load of trust in something that is misguided. An overlooked truism in life is that you can, in fact, be sincerely wrong. You are not saved by your faith; you are saved by the cross. Do I trust my faith or do I trust Jesus?

The third mis-definition of faith is a bit tricky; it's the error that I am saved because I believe. Time out; I can hear my readers screaming and hollering while I write this, but hang on for just a minute. Now I must jump on the semantically exact horse for a second. You did not "earn" your salvation because you are among those that have believed that the Bible is true. Your "faith" did not put you in a separate category. James addresses this intellectual alignment with the Bible.

"You believe that there is one God. Good! Even the demons believe that—and shudder."[73]

Faith is not believing the Bible is true, nor is correct doctrine the key, both are a great start, but it only gets you halfway there. Biblical faith is much more. It's not enough to acknowledge that Jesus is the Savior rather saving faith states; Jesus is my Savior.

Faith can clearly be a fig leaf if you don't get this right. In fact, defining saving faith is exactly what this chapter and the next chapter are all about. And to drive home the point; it's all about the object of your faith; faith in faith or faith in Christ or yet better; trust in self or trust in Christ.

Biblical faith is a personal response to the clear, overwhelming and compelling evidence that Jesus is exactly who He says He is; the Messiah, the Savior of the world, the Way, the Truth and the Life.[74] Personally, claiming and trusting in what He did is the essential point here.

Therefore, He is the one that makes people righteous by what theologians call "imputed righteousness". I did not make myself righteous because I believed rather, I am righteous because I trust and

---

[73] James 2:19

[74] John 14:6

rely on the finished work of the cross. Jesus not only forgives via the cross but also makes people righteous. There are many verses in the New Testament that point to this great truth, but the following verse is called the "great exchange". Sinners are clearly made righteous by the cross.

"God made him who had no sin to be sin for us, so that in him we might become the righteousness of God."[75]

Some might play the "majoring on the minor" card, getting excited about a single verse that supports a pet doctrine. I don't think so; let's look at several more key verses to prove this point.

"But now he has reconciled you by Christ's physical body through death to present you holy in his sight, without blemish and free from accusation."[76]

"...and to present her (believers) to himself as a radiant church, without stain or wrinkle or any other blemish, but holy and blameless."[77]

"because by one sacrifice he has made perfect forever those who are being made holy."[78]

"And so Jesus also suffered outside the city gate to make the people holy through his own blood."[79]

The trust of the New Testament is that believers are made holy via the cross. The Perfect Priest, offers the Perfect Sacrifice that is the Perfect Solution to make people perfect. Imputed righteousness is not an obscure doctrine, it's the backbone of the Gospel.

---

[75] 2 Corinthians 5:21

[76] Colossians 1:22

[77] Ephesian 5:27

[78] Hebrews 10:14

[79] Hebrews 13:12

Now onto the final point; faith in self.

As a teacher in the church, I often ask a very diagnostic question. I use it so often that I fear that it will one day lose its potency, but that seems like a very distant future from the responses I get. The question is by no means original on my part and kudos to the one who came up with it, but here it is: "If you were to die right now and find yourself at the Pearly Gates, and you are asked the question why should you be allowed in?" What will your answer be?

I have been a good person.

I have gone to church regularly.

I have been baptized.

I have faith.

I have been kind to the poor.

I save stray kittens.

I give money to the church.

Note that they all start with "I", your solution, your effort. Your answer reveals who you actually rely on to get through the Pearly Gates, and in many cases, it reveals the fig leaf of self-reliance. The Apostle Paul responds with the counter intuitive.

> *That I may gain Christ, and be found in Him not having a righteousness of my own that comes from the Law but that which is through faith in Christ, the righteousness that comes from God and is by faith."*[80]

Just prior to this, Paul lists his impressive resume' of religious heritage, training, zeal and accomplishments prior to his conversion. If anyone had the impetus to trust in self, it would be Paul, but he calls all his fig

---

[80] Philippians 3:9

leaves "a pile of poop"[81] in light of the cross. His eternal destiny has been entirely entrusted to Christ; his confidence is only in the finished work of the cross. He depends on his Lord and Savior Jesus. Like a parachutist; all or nothing, all in on Jesus and the finished work of the cross or all in on your performance and religion. Paul completely rejects the false security that performance and religious "faith" offer; both are fig leaves. The choice is clear to him, trust in your ability to fly or trust in the parachute.

So, let's be clear about the roles here as we sum things up. The Gospel is not about me, it's about Him. He made me righteous, I did not make myself righteous, by either my deeds or faith. So, who do I trust? Faith in self or faith in Jesus? I trust and rely on Him alone to get me through the Pearly Gates.

OK, I have the theory down, but that is just a start. The raging fires of reality will shake me to the core and reveal who I really trust, me or Jesus. In an all or nothing scenario, my trust in my merit or my trust in the cross is laid bare. I crash to the ground hard. This is what is required to purge meritocracy from my brain and eradicate the remnants of the broken Gospel of "saved by grace, walk by works" from my depraved mind. I stand before God by only the cross, and once I wrap my brain around this, only then, does my life stabilize.

---

[81] Philippians 3:8 a rare use of a vulgar hyperbole by the Apostle Paul to emphasize a point. It is often toned down in English Translation

THE SAND

I remember it was a sunset on a beach in Southern California when I first wrestled with what theologians' call "imputed righteousness". I had been a Christian for some six years now, and regularly spent time with God reading His Word. My guess would be that, at this point in time, I had read the Old Testament 2-3 times and the New Testament 5-6 times. I do not share this to toot my own horn as they say, but rather to illustrate some inherent weaknesses and limitations in my life. Being an introverted, relationally illiterate, prosopagnosic[82], reading his Word was about all that I could do. So that is what I did, and to be real I am indeed truly fascinated by God's Word.

The foundational concept of an imputed righteousness, found in the New Testament will set the stage for a personal revelation that will turn my Christianity on it's head. It is the central theme of the New Testament, and I will get a firsthand glimpse of what the Apostle Paul calls a "righteousness that is by faith."[83] As I wrap my brain around

---

[82] Medical term for "face blind" I have this in spades

[83] Romans 1:17

this life-altering truth, it becomes clear that this is a key foundational reality of the Gospel. My glimpse morphs into the bedrock of my faith as this big picture truth further unfolds from the Bible.

Loneliness so deep that it physically hurt was a pain that was all too common of an experience for me. Rejected, bullied and discarded for most of my early life, I did the only logical thing when I graduated from college; I joined the US Marine Corps. Consequently, my toes squeezed the sand on the beach of US Marine Corps Base, Camp Pendleton on the coast of California. Waves crashing and a typical inspiring sunset, it was a perfect setting for reflection. I had just spent six months doing a deep dive into the Book of Romans. My world was getting turned upside down with the words that were written almost 2000 years ago by the Apostle Paul.

What? Hold the phone! Back up the truck! You joined the Marines? How is that a logical life choice? Again, bullied and discarded in high school, the Marines offered the perfect defense mechanism; be tough. I excelled in the Marines. I was an honor graduate in Officer Candidate School. I also earned the top spot in my Basic Officer Class for military skills. I volunteered to serve as an infantry officer, one of the toughest jobs in the Corps; ready to lead troops in battle against the dreaded Ivan of the Cold War. I eventually achieved a coveted position of being a Recon Platoon Commander (the elite unit within the Corps). I achieved the highest level of physical fitness and qualified high expert in both rifle and pistol. I became someone that people should not mess with anymore. Driven by dedication to my country? Hogwash. I was rather driven by a massive inferiority complex. My unconscious goal was to become a person that people no longer preyed on, and it worked.

This mixed motive paralleled my spiritual walk as I wrestled with this "righteousness by faith" that the Apostle Paul writes about in Romans. Shoes in my hand and sand between my toes, my Christianity was a house of cards that had just imploded.

It needs to be understood that, on the outside, one can appear to excel in a noble pursuit, but on the inside, be driven by less-than-ideal motives, many times compelled by unconscious notions. Thus, it's easy to fool others and it is also easy to fool oneself. My accomplishments in the military closely paralleled my involvement in a collegiate ministry in New York. I led Bible studies, led worship, and was a student leader. And to be fair, God in his sovereignty, used these things to heal and shape me and others; His Word will not return to Him empty[84] It will accomplish something even though my end was marked by fumbling and bumbling. Leading worship especially, buried the needle on the fumble meter in that category, I am just not a music person.

However, there remained an unanswered, "what now?" void in the "Say a prayer, be good and go to heaven" Gospel that I initially clung to. Good for salvation for sure, but my lack of understanding of foundational theology was subsequently filled with convenient and abundant rumor theology. My theology became polluted by cheap performance-based fig leaves for several years and a purging was long overdue. A reboot on steroids was in order, my theology needed to be raked over the coals to get me back on track.

Now before people start screaming and hollering about the fine points of salvation doctrine, let me definitively state, for the record, that the very Son of God connected with me and became my Lord and Savior in early March of 1980. He allowed me to understand the Gospel that I overheard being explained to someone else. Yes, I was initially a lost cause even to Christians. The guy they preached to dragged me along because misery loves company, but I overheard two important things. First, I heard that I was separated from God because of sin. Christ's death on the cross takes away that sin and I could now know God. That seems so simple, but I never comprehended this before, that an obstacle, once removed, allows change, duh. Second, I heard that the Holy Spirit could make you a new person from the inside out. Hello! You have my attention! Deeply terrified by who I was and desperate for a new life, where do I sign? I was invited to a group meeting later that week. I went and that is where I heard for the first time, that God loved me and that proof of this was the fact that His Son died for me.

---

[84] Isaiah 55:11

Now the very Son of God will not die for someone with an ulterior motive. So, God's first words to my stone-cold, dead heart were "I love you". It was clearly an irrefutable fact. Panicked by this truth, I slipped out of the meeting when it was over, and I literally ran. My head was spinning from this revelation. Then God seemed like a gentle whisper in my ear, "Now or never, choose tonight". At the base of an ash tree, on a college campus in upstate New York, on the shore of Lake Ontario, the All-Powerful Risen Christ gave me new life that night. Without a doubt, saying yes to that whisper, was the singular most important decision in my entire life. Nothing else even remotely approaches its significance.

A dramatic conversion and early success in a collegiate ministry, how can this be a house of cards? Fig leaves. I started my walk with Christ, as many do with a misunderstanding; I was genuinely saved but misdirected. I believed that to continue my new acceptance by God, my performance as a Christian was the key. Works righteousness polluted my theology, and my growth plateaued to the level of my ability. I had a shaky foundation at best.

"Commitment", "dedication", "conviction" are all terms thrown around in the church today. All are good terms, and to be clear, all can be the key for breaking from the lures of the world and focusing on Christ. But if one is not careful, it can lead to a precarious position of what I will call "The Christian Moralist". This is the partial Gospel of "saved by grace, walk by works". This is a cleanup your act gospel, walk the line. I know I am going to step on some theological toes here. Yes, you are saved, however transformation is limited to your effort and assurance is results based. You only get so far with this sugar-coated legalism. A full understanding of the Scriptures makes the difference between this being a treadmill of activity with limited progress or a stepping stone to a genuine walk with God.

Driven by anguish to put as much distance between my former life and my new life, I slipped into my default setting of the fig leaves of self-righteousness and my early spiritual successes, based on my desperation, became assurance. I looked down on less committed Christians. The fallacy of trying to earn your salvation by works seems obvious to many believers, but equally fool hardy is trying to maintain your standing by works. This error of religion, which is made by multitudes, is an easy misbelief, of which I also fell for hook, line and sinker. I was doing fine, feeling good, but my faith in performance came crashing down in California when I had my Bathsheba[85] event. A catastrophic moral failure, far from my finest hour, my honor as a Christian man was in shambles, my walk with Him in ruins. I was no longer undefeated in this faith game. I became like Christians I labeled as "uncommitted". I crashed hard and was in flames.

Saturated in the Book of Romans for half a year, Paul's words about a righteousness by faith; a righteousness that is given to me, took on a new clarity. Not my performance, not my effort, not by fig leaves, but rather, by the finished work of the cross.

> *"But now a righteousness from God apart from the law has been made known...this righteousness from God comes through faith in Jesus Christ to all who believe... and are justified freely by his grace through the redemption that came through Christ Jesus"*[86]

God no longer holds out garments of animal skins to cover my shame like he did for Adam, but rather, a robe of righteousness. My sin and shame exchanged for Christ's righteousness.[87] The deal of a lifetime, sealed by faith, this robe of Christ's righteousness, when put on, "hurls all our iniquities into the depths of the sea",[88] "as far as the east is from the west",[89] and, at this point, I desperately needed to rid myself of failure and shame. The cross's forgiveness is not just a one time "get out of jail free" card for the repentant sinner, but forgiveness is also the substance of our position before God as Christians. Grace is what

---

[85] 2 Samuel 11 records this epic moral failure of King David; adultery, murder and cover up. I will not address the specifics of my failure, moral failure is moral failure.

[86] Romans 3:21-24

[87] 2 Corinthians 5:21

[88] Micah 7:19

[89] Psalm 103:12

saved me in the first place, grace is now what also sustains me. Time to button my robe up and tie a sash around my waist. No longer clad in fig leaves, but rather the very righteousness of Christ. Time to fulfill my privilege of bearing God's image and goodness in a fallen world; time to start growing for real. Forget the fig leaves of performance, henceforth; saved by grace, walk by grace.

But was this for real? Was I understanding this correctly? Can I, a failed Christian, claim this? The answer is made clear by the Apostle Paul, he explains to Christians in Romans 8:1:

> *"Therefore, there is now no condemnation for those who are in Christ Jesus."*[90]

Romans 4:7-8:

> *"Blessed are they whose transgressions are forgiven, whose sins are covered. Blessed is the man whose sin the Lord will never count against him."*

Romans 4:5

> *"However, to the man who does not work, but trusts God who justifies the wicked, his faith is credited as righteousness."*

Romans 5:8 drives this concept home with a sledgehammer:

> *"But God demonstrates His own love for us in this: While we were still sinners, Christ died for us. Since we have now been justified by His blood, how much more shall we be saved from God's wrath through Him! For if, while we were God's enemies, we were reconciled to Him through the death of his Son, how much more, having been reconciled, shall we be saved through His life!"*

---

[90] Romans 8:1

Let's unpack that last verse in Romans 5. Grace saved us, grace also sustains us. We got a truckload of grace when we were literally His enemies. Now that we are his kids...we're now talking pipeline. Have you internalized this? Do you fully believe that you are 100% righteous? Righteous not by your works and performance but a righteousness that has been credited (imputed) to you. A simple test brings who you truly trust to light. When you sin, do you run away from God, like Adam hiding in the garden, or do you run to Him?

My moralist model of Christianity crumbled under the repeated hammering of Scriptural truths. The Gospel continued to unfold and every revelation revealed an amazing God. How far I have fallen is staggering. How much restoration is needed is humbling.

Paul lays out this astonishing truth to Christians in Colossians 1:21-22:

"Once you were alienated from God and were enemies in your minds because of your evil behavior. But now He has reconciled you by Christ's physical body through death to present you holy in His sight, without blemish and free from accusation."

Before I introduce this verse to my discipleship students I ask, "By a show of hands, who can say they are holy in His sight, without a blemish and free from any accusation?" No one raises their hand. This imputed righteousness, a righteousness that is given, a righteousness by faith is fundamental to walking with Christ, yet few grasp it. Paul shows that this is indeed a fundamental truth, in the next verse he writes, "This is the Gospel".

If you asked me that question when I was a student leader in college, I would not have raised my hand because I trusted in my performance fig leaves as a Christian. Now I stand and raise my hand. In fact, I will not even for a New York nanosecond stand before God trusting in my own righteousness, but I will entirely and absolutely stand exclusively on the righteousness of Christ that has been simply given to me. This is what I now steadfastly trust. Not just for salvation but also for sustaining my daily walk with God. His righteousness is complete and absolute, nothing else matters. My Savior is Jesus, not me.

Christ's righteousness has been given to you if you have claimed it by faith. The New Testament refers to all Christians as "Saints". Not by effort and performance, but by his work on the cross. I am 100% righteous! I won the lottery! Time to start living like I have indeed won the lottery, and it is also time to stop buying lottery tickets, to try and win something I already have.

Paul takes the first 11 chapters in Romans to make a very clear case for this "righteousness by faith". What should our response be? Well, let's look at the beginning of chapter 12:

> *"Therefore, I urge you, brothers and sisters, in view of God's mercy, to offer your bodies as a living sacrifice, holy and pleasing to God—this is your spiritual act of worship. Do not conform any longer to the pattern of this world, but be transformed by the renewing of your mind. Then you will be able to test and approve what God's will is—his good, pleasing and perfect will."*[91]

Gods' complete forgiveness is not a license to sin nor diplomatic immunity to do whatever you want. It's rather an opportunity to live the life you were created for. Also note, that understanding God's mercy (chapters 1-11) proceeds a genuinely changed life (chapter 12-15). Please also note how dying to self-supremacy is the key response to internalizing the supremacy of Christ, it's called a "living sacrifice". Obedience is a response to grace, and a path to healing, not a means to gain or retain God's favor. Read Romans again if there is any question.

Wait a second, it can't be that simple. It is, think about the original plan. Adam and Eve had everything, God's blessing, inheritance, dominion over the Earth, fellowship with God, eternal life. The question is begged; what did they do to deserve all this? The answer is absolutely nothing, they were born into it. But we lost it all when we subscribed to self-supremacy. Repentance reverses this as we die to

---

[91] Romans 12:1-3

self and replace self-supremacy with the supremacy of Christ. As a result, we can likewise be reborn into the covenant of God's family, and as sons and daughters, share in the family's wealth and have everything else restored just like the prodigal son. The cost however is enormous, the Father gave His only Son. The Son endured the cross to blow the hinges off the door. We leave everything to walk through it. The entire universe is focused on this portal and reconnection with God, there's nothing else, that even remotely matters.

My anchor relationship in my life is with my Heavenly Father, my connection to Him is based on the finished work of the cross. My own righteousness, utterly worthless and now obviously unreliable, is no longer what I depend on for God's favor and acceptance. Realizing the complete forgiveness in Christ; past, present and future, I shake the California sand from my feet and put on my shoes…time to walk with Christ in a new chapter.

From that day forward my walk with Christ, though rebuilt on a new and trustworthy foundation of grace, is with a limp. My limp reminds me of what I was saved from. My limp reminds me that I have nothing to go back to. My limp reminds me that His grace is sufficient for me. My limp reminds me that His power is made perfect in my weakness.[92] So limp onward I go, it's my only option.

My relationship with my Heavenly Father is now fully grace based, not ever again to be performance based. My connection to Jesus, the True Vine, is likewise grace based. No longer do I merit any standing before God with my performance. I have favor with God, but it is entirely unmerited; this is the very definition of grace. Likewise, I can no longer complain, label or look down on and criticize other people. My relationship with people is likewise compelled to be clearly grace based. Grace is the paradigmatic shift needed to selflessly walk with God and love people. The fragility of performance righteousness, now obvious, illuminates this.

The imputed righteousness of Christ is all I have.

---

[92] 2 Corinthians 12:9-10

All dysfunction in human relationships seem to stem from errant theology and application. Self-supremacy or pride is at the root of all this. If my relationship with God is poisoned by performance-based thinking, this toxin will pollute my relationships with people as well. People's shortfalls will frustrate, annoy and hurt me, but unconditional agape' love does not depend on this, grace is unmerited favor…I get it now, UNMERITED. Humility and dying to self as a response to God's grace is the foundation for a truly transformed life. This is a change in the fabric of my being. No longer do I try to score points to impress God or put on a superficial religious persona to impress people, but rather I am given a new spirit and a new heart[93], where things are real. This is in fact God's plan for restoration, returning to the original created order; love God, love people. The original foundation of all this remains unchanged; unmerited, grace based, agape love.

I need to trust in grace, not my effort. This necessary prerequisite enables me to love God and love people and to enjoy the community of believers and the presence of God. The key concept of; "God opposes the proud but gives grace to the humble", places humility as the portal through which I must pass in order to know God. The Bible calls this "dying to self". Paul nails it; once again we revisit Galatians 3:20:

> *"I have been crucified with Christ and I no longer live, but Christ lives in me. The life I live in the body, I live by faith in the Son of God, who loved me and gave Himself for me."*

"Are you so dull?"[94] Jesus queries his disciples after years of being with Him. "Yes," I answer. Likewise walking with Christ for years, my intellect misfires on a regular basis. Please God have patience, I am an idiot, teach me. My comprehension of righteousness eludes me as does my execution. I am not getting this. Stalled for years at this

---

[93] Ezekiel 36:26

[94] Mark 7:18

impasse, a career change positions me to get back on track, and yes again it hurts. Electric shocks and small explosions fuel the next tier of understanding the Gospel. Time to revisit the basics, time to revisit the cross.

THE GROUND ROD

I am an electrician, it is a good job, pays well and is both mentally and physically challenging. It warrants serious consideration for the younger crowd searching for a career path. Certainly not the astronaut path we aspired to when we were kids, but a practical, respectable job. Now, one of the cool benefits about this trade is you get to use techno-babble terms like "Grounding Electrode Conductor". It makes one appear uber cool, but the reality is that this is just a wire, certainly nothing to write home to mom about. However, jargon like this is effective in creating the illusion of professionalism when dealing with mere mortals.

So, let's throw in another cool term; "fault current". This is fancy talk used by the practitioners of the electrical arts to describe an unintended electric current that can shock people or start fires. Something has gone wrong to create a fault current, hence the name. They taught us very complex things in electrician school, such as fire, smoke and shocking people are bad and that electricians should avoid making the mistakes that create such possibilities. Licensed electricians rarely do such things but nevertheless, other factors such as physical damage, faulty components, water, and rework by unqualified people can create a myriad of problems. The key thing is to drive any fault current into the ground, so the circuit breaker can trip and shut off the power, rendering the situation safe.

If you ever had occasion to observe your electrical wiring in your house, you would have noticed a bare or green wire at every switch, outlet and junction box. This bare wire is the parallel system that is commonly referred to as the "ground", and it exists only for one purpose; to facilitate driving any fault current to the ground. Every one of those bare wires are tied together and culminates in a single wire that connects to a ground rod pounded into your yard. Yes, you probably guessed it, that single wire is called the "Grounding Electrode Conductor". It is the most important wire in the whole system. It must be a certain size, color, and connected by specific means. A ton of rules associated with this, because it is the most important wire in the system. It is the key to getting the fault current safely to the ground rod and keeping people from being hurt.

Without diving into the cool science behind this strategy, which most mortals fail to comprehend, I can basically sum up the reason why this works is because of the enormous mass of the Earth. Take all the electricity ever created in history and drive it into the earth and it would not have the slightest effect. Like spitting in the ocean, the enormity of the planet means, that for all intents and purposes, the planet can absorb an infinite amount of electricity.

So, it is with the cross. The perfect life of the Son of God, when put into the equation, can absorb all the faults and sins of every man, woman and child that ever has or will live. His righteousness, forgiveness and unconditional love is just that massive. I have mentioned that I am not a Bible scholar, and at times, I confess that I struggle to wrap my brain around this, but it is clear from Scripture that this is indeed the case. The imperative is not that I fully understand it, but rather I fully embrace it. My sin debt is staggering in its magnitude. Spending forever in Hell will not pay it off. It has crushed my life and my eternity. It's a giant that blocks the only way to return to God. My choice is that I can bear that debt, or Jesus can do it for me. The choice is mine. Faith or trust is the all-important conductor that drives all my sin debt into the ground rod which is the wooden cross at Calvary. Once connected to the cross by this trust, the guilt, shame and penalty for all my past, present and future sin is gone.[95] Not only forgiven, but also made 100% righteous.

In America we have a strong tendency to adhere to mis-gospels. Gospels that sound correct but are fundamentally flawed in some way so that they are powerless to save or powerless to genuinely transform. Rumor theology fuels this poison; the antidote is the truth about grace. The one I fell for is the "saved by grace, walk by works" teaching. We are genuinely saved, but then fall back on maintaining our position before God by our performance. The book of Galatians speaks to this misbelief of the Christian Moralist.[96] This meritocracy mindset lays the foundation to an often-misunderstood trap called "legalism".

Jesus clearly warned us about being on your guard against this "yeast (teaching) of the Pharisees".[97] This is the mindset of legalism, aka, "works righteousness". I like to call it "fig leaves", mostly because it is a cool book title, but more importantly, it is a tensioned theme that starts in Genesis where the stage is set, and the drama follows through the entire Bible all the way to Revelation. Works righteousness keeps billions from realizing that the grace found in the cross is the only way to connect with the Father.[98]

My pride, my efforts, my self-reliance, my faith in self, has thwarted my transformation as a Christian because it poisoned my connection to Christ. The fault current of pride, in turn, energized various aspects of my life and when people got close to me, they got shocked and hurt.

This is definitely a spectrum disorder for all of God's people. This side of glory every Christian wrestles with this concept. It is simply a matter

---

[95] Colossians 2:14

[96] Galatians 3:1-6

[97] Matthew 16:6

[98] John 14:6

of degree and is inversely proportional to how much you have died to self. The "tell" here is obvious; dysfunctional relationships with people reflects a dysfunctional relationship with God. A performance-based relationship with God morphs into a performance-based relationship with people. Hurts, anger and frustrations with people is the norm. But a grace-based relationship with God is indicated by grace-based relationships with people. Love, joy, peace, patience, kindness, goodness, faithfulness, gentleness and self-control, are the fruits[99] and positive relational terms that point to the "spot on" theology of grace. There is a reason why every command in the New Testament to forgive others is always coupled with "as Christ forgave you". You must be grounded in the forgiveness of the cross to forgive and be patient with others. You must be grounded in grace to functionally relate to others.

All of Paul's letters in the New Testament start off with "Grace and peace to you" and end with a similar blessing. It behooves us to ask why? Grace, by definition, is "unmerited favor", this is the core of God's unconditional, "agape'" love (a Greek word). This is contrary to "legalism". Legalism is a mindset that thinks that our favor or our standing before God is based on our performance (conditional). Do good and God loves and rewards you, do bad and God whacks you. Legalism really does not have anything to do with the presence or absence of rules as is often taught, but rather the motive for adhering to the rules. If your mind set is, God accepts me because I obey the rules, you have misunderstood something very fundamental in your walk with Christ. These fig leaves of effort and performance leave us insecure in our relationship with God and like Adam, hiding in the garden, we often become fearful and alienated. This is often a new concept for many, and in some readers, no doubt, gears are grinding as a paradigmatic shift in your theology begins.

The legalists are always in conflict with the gospel of grace. Note how many times in the New Testament the Apostle Paul mentions his conflict with the Jews and the legalistic "circumcision group" (those that

[99] Galatians 5:22-23

advocate performance). I always laugh a bit when Paul is so frustrated with the legalist, that preach circumcision, that he vents in his letter to the Galatian church; "As for those agitators, I wish they would go the whole way and emasculate themselves!"[100] Yes, you read that right, he wants them to go ahead and cut their junk off, lock, stock and barrel.

You probably looked that verse up to check on my accuracy, good for you. Now flip back a page or two and read what Paul says about Hagar and Sarah at the end of chapter 4. Abraham, the father of all the Jews, had two sons; Isaac and Ishmael. Ishmael was born by impregnating his wife's slave Hagar (BTW this was by his wife's request).[101] Ishmael represents works righteousness, and he persecuted Isaac who was born later by Abraham's wife, Sarah. Isaac, on the other hand, represents God's child born by His promised miracle. Note the conflict between reliance on self and reliance on God's promise. Let's also be very clear that this is not my wacky interpretation, this is actually the Apostle Paul's interpretation.[102]

This theme finds continuity even in Isaac's kids. Jacob and Esau battled in the womb, two groups representing, works verses grace. Throughout Scripture we can see evidence of the two schools of thought conflicting with each other, works verses grace. Every relationship we have is either grace based, or performance based. Our theology determines this, our theology reveals this. Our theology is the foundation of every relationship we have. Our theology reveals relationships characterized by peace or relationships characterized by frustration. Our theology is laid bare by our lives.

I struggle deeply with this tension of meritocracy and grace. For decades, it's been drilled into my head that that acceptance by others is based entirely on what I do. Peers, family and authorities seem to universally require correct performance in order to be approved. It's the way of the world. Screw up and words of anger, fists and even

---

[100] Galatians 5:12 this is hyperbole, not to be taking literally.

[101] Things were different back then

[102] Galatians 4:21-31

bullets fly. Our conflict and tension with people are rooted in our pride. Even to this day I still wrestle with this for this is all I have ever known. It was only natural to extend this harmful ideology to my relationship with God.

Bear in mind that bad theology pollutes every human relationship we have, as well as our relationship with God. This is the common experience of humanity, especially if you come from an unbelieving family like mine. Breaking from this is nothing short of impossible without the power of the Holy Spirit. However the truth of Scripture paints a different picture of God's love being absolutely unconditional, God's forgiveness is not earned. Because of the cross, it is simply offered and simply accepted. A righteousness that is bestowed is beyond comprehension, but it is clear from the Bible that this is indeed the case. This mind-blowing grace is only the beginning of things. Saved by grace, walk by grace, this is the theology that my life is now based on.

So, it's completely normal to be confused at this time. If I am forgiven and accepted by God, the question is begged, why then do I have to obey? But also, why are there still so many rules in the New Testament if my relationship with God is not based on what I do? The watch dogs of "cheap grace" and "the seeker sensitive Gospel", likewise are no doubt getting wrapped around the axle about now. I get it, I had those same exact thoughts well up in my brain as the imputed righteousness of the cross came to the fore front of my thinking. But God, being ever so faithful, provided lessons that brought key Scriptures to light as comprehension of this issue was skillfully woven into my walk with Him. The next two chapters are those lessons, they both physically hurt, one much more than the other. So please pay attention I do not wish to repeat them.

THE RULES

Once again, I found myself emerging from a state of unconsciousness. I stared at the very clear blue sky of the Mojave Desert, my eyes struggled to align and focus. I was lying flat on my back, in the middle of the road, the intense pain of an epic bicycle crash just a minute or so ago had not caught up with my body yet. Pain and a lot of it, was penciled in to arrive in short order. The wipeout scored an 8.6 out of 10 on the crash-o-meter (a personal record that stands to this day). I went through the familiar check list; wiggled the toes…check, wiggled the fingers…left check, right…nothing worked, possible spinal injury. I will just lay still for a minute or two and wait for the world to stop spinning.

John Butterworth, aka "The Butterman", was an accomplished triathlete. He was also my roommate and a fellow infantry officer. I was his training partner, even though he ran and cycled me into the dirt. His response to my protests to accompany him on training runs and cycling jaunts was a simple, "you are the only one who can keep up with me". As such, we found ourselves driving out to the middle of the Mojave Desert one winter's day, trying to knock out about a hundred miles on our bicycles before lunch on a lonely back road. We parked at a place called "Scissors Crossing" in Anza Borrego State

Park. A cop manning a speed trap watched us unload our bikes that morning. We exchanged a friendly wave.

About thirty miles into the ride, after a very long climb, came the adrenaline-charged downhill bombing. Keep in mind that the Butterman was training for a race, so he was working on speed technique. I barely kept up with him, having busted a lung about halfway up, and as a result, I was a few hundred feet behind him.

The Butterman was bombing down this mountain so fast that he started to overtake a car ahead of him, so in a sharp left-hand curve he applied the brakes to avoid an unsafe situation. Bad call, never brake in a turn, because the physics are tricky. Brake before and you are OK, but brake aggressively in a turn and you will probably not fare well, especially when there is loose sand on the road's shoulder. The Butterman was probably pushing 45 mph when he lost it. He put forth a valiant effort to recover from the death wobble, but in the end, he was bested by the forces at play and the Butterman went down in a hard spinning slide. Not a particularly pleasant turn of events for the Butterman.

Likewise, I was bombing down the aforementioned mountain road myself, desperately trying to close the gap with the legendary Butterman. Distracted by the spectacle before me, it suddenly occurred to me that I was going to ride into his yard sale in a matter of seconds at a very high rate of speed. I instinctively braked hard, forgetting the rule of not braking in a turn, and my fate was sealed. I headed for a solid rock wall about 6 feet high, cut into the side of the mountain to make a road. "Oh man! This was going to hurt," was my last thought, as bicycle, Blombo and bedrock met in a violent collision.

A reconstruction of the events revealed the following: my high-performance bicycle which I spent two months' salary on, was a pretzel 50 feet uphill from my final resting spot in the middle of the road. The Butterman told me he turned his attention to my fate when he heard the gunshot like sound of my 140-psi racing tire blow upon impact. He watched me hit the wall and "tomahawk" through cactus and rock, then down the wall and came to rest where I laid, in the middle of the road, staring at the blue sky. Emerging from unconsciousness, I laid still; zero movement was justified at that time. The familiar face of my roommate entered my field of view.

"Blombo…you OK?"

"No…I think I broke my arm."

"Can you move it?"

"No….. give me a minute."

No immediate action was warranted by the Butterman at that time. His infantry officer compassion for others was reflected by his comment, "That's not too bad" as he walked away to tend to the matter at hand. We both struggled to regroup from our shattered circumstance. My concern for him was equal; no doubt he had road rash of epic proportions, but since he was ambulatory, he likewise was, "not too bad". This is how Marine Infantry Officers think, "a little bit of pain never hurt anyone".

A broken arm is serious, but manageable. A spinal injury, however, was still a possibility and it haunted me. After laying, there for a few minutes, my soundness of mind, my ability to focus my eyes and movement of my right arm returned. It was not broken after all, and the spinal injury also got ruled out. Well, that was a plus and I struggled to sit up. Water bottles, tire pumps, and bike parts, were strewn on the road. Thirty miles from our car, in the middle of nowhere, we found ourselves in a bad way. The bleeding and limping Butterman approached after clearing things from the road.

"Can you get up?"

"I'll give it a try."

The Butterman extended a helpful hand, and I struggled to my feet.

We sat on the side of the road pondering our fate and what our next move would be. Pain was entering the equation now; my right shoulder had moved from numb and lifeless to hurts like all get out. The pain train had arrived and so to focus my attention on something else, I removed my helmet.

The large dents the rock made in the helmet were obvious. I hit the rock with my helmet and right shoulder as my momentum hurled me over the handlebars. Knocked unconscious, I do not remember anything between "Oh man!" and blue sky. My injuries were relatively minor compared to the magnitude of the crash. I credit three things for this: Dumb luck, (a proclivity of mine), excellent physical conditioning (thanks to the Marine Corps) and the helmet that the Butterman talked me into buying just two weeks earlier.[103] Not wanting to look "uncool", I was the last holdout in our cycling group to buy this essential piece of protective equipment. Finally caving in, this purchase just spared me from a traumatic brain injury. My mental capacity reasonably intact, thanks to my friend, we sat on the side of the road. As we took a drink from our water bottles, a motor home slowly climbed up the mountain road and stopped in front of us.

Power window hummed down, and a friendly voice inquired, "You guys OK?"

"We have had better days."

"Looks like you guys could use a lift."

"Are you heading for Scissors Crossing?

"Yes."

What remained of our high-performance bicycles were handed up, via human chain, to the luggage rack on top of the motor home. We entered the climate controlled inside and rested on the bench seats of the kitchen table in the rear, as the motor home continued its journey towards Scissors Crossing. Retired Mom and Dad were in the front seats and adult son was in the back with us. We regaled him with the tale of our misfortune. His response was simple, "Sounds like you two could use some cold beer". In all my life a cold beer has yet to hit the spot like that one did. We unloaded our mangled bikes at our car, thanked our Good Samaritans and parted company. The Cop emerged from his speed trap and approached.

"Those bikes looked a whole lot nicer when you left", he commented, in the dry humor that cops are known for. A brief recounting of our tale and we talked him into taking a photo of us and our bikes, bloodied

---

[103] Cut me a bit of slack here, real bicycle helmets were just being introduced to the cycling community at this time (1986ish) replacing the legacy leather helmets that were practically worthless..

and mangled, the photo reminds me of the day when I learned about rules.

The nonsense rumor theology that needs to be addressed is the oft-heard statement describing Christianity; "It's not a bunch of rules…it's a relationship". Now put your screaming and hollering on hold for just a minute. Let me be clear: Christianity is indeed a relationship. In fact, this is one of the key dimensions of the Gospel that is often missing. We are redeemed from the penalty of sin (this is often where the "Get out of Hell Gospel", when preached, stops, and we are genuinely reconciled to God. The latter being the essence of the "relationship, not a religion" that we address. That part being true, we become a bit befuddled when we see tons of rules in the New Testament. So, what gives? The missing ingredient is restoration.

The Biblical objective of God's Spirit is to empower us, to not only declare the Gospel but to also demonstrate its power via our lives. Clearly the message is always tied to the messenger. In order to be believable, those that bear His name and proclaim His Gospel, must bear it with some measure of newness of life, genuine joy, and most of all; selfless agape' love.

We must grasp that God's intent is to restore us to our original condition where we selflessly love Him and others. There is a heap load of transformation that needs to take place, much of which will not happen this side of eternity, but Jesus is indeed in the life changing business, and He is eager to get started. His role, via the Spirit, is akin to the role of a coach, the RSV[104] calls Him a counselor in John 16. Guess what, coaches and counselors have rules. Not to qualify or disqualify us, but rather to protect and enable us.

The rule in cycling is to always wear a helmet. I resisted compliance to this protective rule for quite some time until my friend, operating in the role of a coach, went zero tact to penetrate my knuckleheadedness, to get me to do the obvious, "Blombo, don't be

---

[104] Revised Standard Version of the Bible, a great translation of the Bible

stupid… buy a helmet". Aware of the message and respecting the messenger, I reluctantly complied. Being a reasonably functional human being today is all due to me obeying the rule of bicycle helmets. Thank God for caring friends, blunt and direct that he was, and rules that protect.

However, there are another bunch of rules with a different purpose. As with many endeavors and sports, I have been involved in, there are tons of rules. These are the rules that enable you. Keeping your eye on the ball, follow through, squeeze the trigger, keep your left arm straight during the back swing, spin the pedals 100 rpms, climb with your feet, sing from your diaphragm, etc, etc, etc. All are rules in various endeavors that help a neophyte slowly transform to a master.

Coaches of all types typically break down, isolate and develop specific skills. Then they combine these fundamental skills into a higher competency. The rules of the New Testament coach are just that. They are like the footprints painted on the floor of the dance school. Generosity is just a portion of being selfless, step 1, being kind is another, step 2, forgiving others step 3, etc, etc. Awkward at first and repeated seemingly endlessly to the student, the dance slowly emerges and soon we keep in step with the rhythm of God's Spirit. But each step is important and must be learned. Frustrating and glacially slow, because there is much damage to undo, we stumble on. Both individuals and the world have been revolutionized by God's people dancing like a 5-year-old. Heaven, of course, is the professional dance troupe.

God is inherently and intensely relational and all the rules of both the Old Testament and New Testament reflect this. It is imperative to understand that the rules not only protect, but they also enable and empower us to function in the selfless agape' relational love we were created for. We must wrap our brains around this essential truth.

But "Religion", the toxin of the legalist, creeps into the church to wreak havoc by choking off this flow of grace and stalling spiritual growth. Here the rules are a twisted means to qualify or disqualify. Often this subtle indication of legalism is unnoticed, hidden under a thin veil of spirituality. The essential theology of grace is the antidote to the toxin of performance religion. So, let's look at some broken Gospels of rumor theology in light of grace.

The Debtor's Gospel: It's foolish to think that we can earn our salvation by good works, but it is equally unsound to try and pay Him back. The cross is not a loan, it's an inheritance. Unfortunately, this subconscious motive is more common than one might think.

The Probationers' Gospel: In this model, the defendant has been found guilty, but the judge is going to give the sinner one more chance to walk the line, screw up and it's into the slammer. This mis-gospel erases past sins, an emotional repentance and a heartfelt "give me one more chance" lends credence to this theological error of trying a second time to earn God's favor. Defeat in the future is inevitable and so many abandon the faith as a result. The Gospel is not probation, it's a dismissal. Forgiveness is complete for past, present and future sins. The law is no longer applicable, it's been canceled. Similar to a discharge from the military, military law is no longer applicable.

The Moralist's Gospel: This is my favorite; I know this one all too well for this was my trap. Saved by grace, walk by works. Like a tire with a slow leak, we have to be diligent to pump good works into our lives to offset the losses; keep the ledger in the black, our assurance before God is based on how good we are. Our connection to God is not temporary foster care, it's a permanent adoption. Similar to the Probationer's Gospel, we constantly ask for forgiveness, so we don't lose our station. This joyless treadmill of performance wears out the sturdiest of people. The inevitable duplicity eventually snuffs out any peace that an imputed righteousness brings and, if not careful, can morph into the worst of all...

The Legalist' Gospel: In its worst form, it's a salvation by works, but more subtly, it's a health and wealth theology of earned "blessings" or moral supremacy. Virtually every religion other than Christianity is marked by a formula of adhering to a moral code. Salvation by works is everywhere. This is the default setting of people, that is why it is so common. Its birth is found in Eden with the fig leaf. For the unsuspecting Christian a sense of superiority can emerge if one is successful at the game of the Moralist. A sense of unworthiness can also predominate if one's life is marked by failure. Christianity is not a contest, it's a covenant. The legalist is simply the model prisoner who relishes his position among the inmates and often morphs into a moral bully.

We are not saved by our obedience to rules, nor does our obedience as believers earn us any special status. An incomplete theology drives us to quickly conclude that obedience to the New Testament rules is, therefore, optional, but that flies in the face of the Lordship of Jesus. We were created to selflessly love others; this is the foundational joy and objective for our lives and pleases both the Father and the Son as their glory is shown to the world.

Step by step we must return to this selfless agape love, in day-to-day practice. After all a fish returned to the water should thrive in its natural environment. Likewise, a soul truly reconciled to God should evidence a life that is fundamentally aligned with its created purpose of loving God and loving people. Obedience, in light of the magnificent grace of God, fuels this. The only thing that counts is faith (in this grace) expressing itself through love.[105] The result of such transformation is an ever-increasing joy in our lives and effectiveness in our witness to an unsaved world. They should want to be like us. Adhere to rules for the wrong reasons and we leave a trail of hurt people in our wake, as we live a joyless life that is a turnoff to the unbelieving world.

The Spirit works in our lives to empower, encourage, energize and enable us to enjoy a life that we were created to live. We are the "imago dei", which is theological babble for the image of God. We need to live like Christ lived. The rules of the New Testament must be understood in this context of restoration.

And guess what? God will use restored people to empower, encourage, energize and enable other people to enjoy their destiny of being the imago dei. Am I using the Bible to club people or am I an agent of change? Holier than thou or imparting life? Contest or covenant? Pride vs humility. Humility and grace are the mark of a disciple of the Risen Christ. Everyone else is just playing church.

---

[105] Galatians 5:6

Grace is our confidence, and grace is also the means of transformation. Our relationship, our connection to Christ is grace based; our connection to people should likewise, be grace based. If you rely on your performance, the toxin of religion and the power of sin will create mayhem in every relationship you have, both with God and with people. A dysfunctional relationship with God carries over to dysfunctional relationships with people. These are indeed interwoven truths. Absolutely every relationship must be graced based. Connect with God via grace, connect with people via grace. Saved by grace, walk by grace.

I wish I could have learned this without slamming into a rock wall at 45 mph; that just flat out hurt.

Ok that last chapter is one I do not want to repeat, but with this new knowledge, the brain housing group[106] erratically fires, trying to reconcile the Old Testament with the New. Again, big picture stuff, but it is essential that I grasp a cohesive fusion of my understanding of the two divisions of the Bible.

But the transitional nature of the law is a point of confusion for me, what's the deal here? Extreme hypothermia puts me in the position to understand this oft-confused dimension of the Scriptures. Follow me to a point of such physiological cold that rational thought is extinct, from there the sacrificial law of the Old Testament makes perfect sense.

---

[106] Marine speak for your head or mind

THE GAME

The temperature hovered around freezing when the day long drizzle transformed into a soul sucking rain. We were tired, cold and totally miserable. Our patrol halted and formed a hasty 360-degree defense, while the patrol leader took a radio call and consulted the map. We laid on the rain-soaked ground defending ourselves against an enemy that we knew was not out there. The weapons are loaded with blanks, this is artificial, this is practice, this is how Marines were trained to fight World War III.

The game was "The Three Day War", the graduating exercise for all officers attending Basic Officer Class[107] at Marine Base Quantico, Virginia. Welcome to Day 1. Every normal human being was inside, warm and dry. Any enemy would react the same way and thus an advantage can be seized by the worst of weather; bayonet the enemy as he warms himself by the fire or huddles in his tent.

Unfortunately, the rain gear we wore, which was affectionately called the "duck suit" was all but worthless. It did not breathe. Thus, our

---

[107] aka The Basic School

sweat saturated the cotton uniforms from the inside; good for about an hour, we had been wearing it for half a day. Cotton is a great fabric for summertime but quite possibly the worst fabric to wear in the cold. Once it gets wet, you are better off buck naked.

A future artillery officer and fellow Christian, Vance Breshears, laid on the muddy ground a few feet from me. He adjusted his helmet and then, so not to break noise discipline, got my attention with a whisper, "Blombo".

I silently and cynically looked his way. I noticed that his perpetual grin was nowhere to be found.

The Vance spoke the truest words I have ever heard uttered by a human, "You know this really sucks".

The needle on the "fun meter" had zeroed out hours ago, it was now registering undisputedly on the "suck-o-meter" and this was just Day 1. Unbeknownst to us, 48 hours later, the bottom would drop out of the suck-o-meter and the game would descend into a mass casualty event for the base. We would medivac around 80 lieutenants due to hypothermia, a third of our strength. One lieutenant would actually flatline due to cardiac arrest; fortunately, he was resuscitated by the heroic efforts of our navy corpsmen and doctors[108].

This was not a case of people feeling a bit of a chill and wanting a cup of hot cocoa or a spot of tea. That milestone passed a long time ago, but, rather, hypothermia is a medical emergency where the body gets so cold it cannot rewarm itself and recovery is impossible without medical intervention. Rational thought evaporates as the central nervous system implodes and the victim, if left alone, irreversibly slides to a certain and cold death in slow motion. The perfect combination of, never give up Marines, lousy gear and prolonged wet and cold was set in motion; we headed for disaster at full speed. My friend had unwittingly uttered this prophetic warning that fell only on deaf ears. The base commander however, eventually played his trump card and pulled the plug on the game after only two and a half days. This would

---

[108] The Marines do not have their own medics but rather rely on the Navy for this. The Navy Marine Corps team is confusing to many

be the only time in my five years as a Marine that I seriously entertained the thought that I might actually die[109].

Day 2, the perpetual rain continued. The M-60 machinegun I lugged around for this game was rightly called "the pig". It consumed so much ammo that it required a three-man team. The pig weighed about 21 pounds empty and as the gunner I carried hundreds of rounds of ammo on top of that, plus a 40-pound pack and 20 pounds of flak jacket and web gear. The ammo bearer simply carried the massive amount of ammo that it ate. The team leader carried the tripod, spare barrel and still more ammo. The pig got very hungry, and its ravenous appetite had to be satisfied. At this time in the fun, hypothermia had claimed dozens, our ammo bearer was amongst them. The team leader and I split up the load of our fallen comrade. A harsh tote for sure but this was what we signed up for and this resolve was clearly needed to defeat Ivan if World War III ever materialized. We must rise to this challenge.

At zero dark thirty, with no sleep, we attacked a nameless hill. The ceaseless, and now freezing rain continued. Pandemonium absolutely dominated the scene as we advanced. Everyone was screaming, hollering and shooting as flares illuminated the objective. I and others remained stationary and unleashed what is called a "base of fire", delivering a high volume of accurate fire. This pins the bad guys down and makes them cry for mommy. What remained of two platoons attacked the flank, where geometry dictates a clear advantage of the flankers over the flanked. In Marine speak, this is called an "envelopment". A lull in the chaos indicated that the "enemy"[110] was playing dead and the mission was accomplished. The signal was given to consolidate on the objective and prepare for a counterattack.

---

[109] It is my understanding that this winter storm killed 14 people, it was nasty.

[110] Fellow Marines using a slightly different uniform play the role of "aggressors" and pretend they get shot

As daylight slowly illuminated the world to the seeing, my next move was obvious; find my team leader. In the dead of the night, he fell into a freezing river and in the chaos he disappeared. Walking the lines, I found him sitting on the ground, leaning back against a tree, he was absolutely devoid of any mental coherency.

"Are you OK?" I asked.

"Thursday." he replied.

"I think not" was my response as I guided and carried him to the medivac site. Hypothermia's grip clearly was dragging another towards death. At the crowded medivac site, the battle raged for others. The ammo may have been blanks but the hypothermia was very real. Dozens fought for their lives. Without intervention, the core temperature of these men would continue to drop until cardiac arrest finished the battle. The tipping point is marked by the cessation of shivering, followed by loss of rational thought and a serious erosion of physical coordination as the central nervous system starts its collapse.

For another half day, and many miles, the never-ending freezing rain continued. Carrying the load of three men and the insufferable cold, sapped the remainder of any capacity I had. Already drained by the load of two men for most of the game, the redline was crossed as the load of three men crushed. The point of no return was hours ago, this was just getting me deeper from where recovery was not possible. How I functioned at any level at this time remains a mystery. I was numb in every sense of the word.

In a short lull of the game, I noticed obvious lapses in my thinking process, this was uncharted territory. Way beyond shivering for hours, I checked for hypothermia by touching each of my fingers sequentially to its thumb, an old mountain climber's trick. It is a very simple demonstration of physical coordination. Anyone can do it, but if you are cold and can't pull it off, your life is on the line, and your ability to make rational decisions is all but gone, this is your last chance to call for help. Index, middle, ring, what was I doing? This was not good. The vestiges of my mental capacity recognized the clear signs of hypothermia, I had only minutes. Soon I would collapse in this forest and a search party of zombies would be dispatched to recover a cold corpse. I deeply dreaded the fact that I was going to die on a stupid training exercise. The inevitable came, unable to call for help, I blacked out, "Sorry mom, I did my best," was my last thought, as I fought an unwinnable battle.

According to my friends, I fortunately remained ambulatory, but like a sleep walker I was completely unaware of anything. My friends found me in a confused state and guided me to the assembly point. We were in a non-tactical formation as the plug was pulled on the game by the base commander. My friends took over, they physically grabbed me and directed me to where I needed to go. I woke up in the hot shower of my room, most of my uniform was still on, my fingers were wrinkled because of how long I was there.[111] I never, ever wanted to play this game again.

Clearly the lesson learned here was that our cold weather gear was totally inadequate. We had not fought a war in the cold since Korea and most of the gear we had seemed to be from that era. Years later, as I departed from active service, uber cool GoreTex® and synthetic performance fabrics started showing up. I like to think that a report of some 80 lieutenants becoming cold casualties in 1984 reached the ears and attention of some brass in Headquarters and got things changed. At a minimum, my respect for the veterans of the “Frozen Chosin” and the “Battle of the Bulge” is nothing short of heroic.

Extreme circumstances, but keep in mind, this was a game, this was not even real. For the record, what I have just described is not even the minor leagues. Combat veterans play hardball in the majors, I became a casualty playing tee ball. Combat vets are the ones that sport the true 1000-yard stare. We definitely got into the triple digits but remained a far cry from the extremes experienced by other veterans. War games are temporary methodology put in place to teach us how to function and fight in a real war. This was just one of many steps to get Marines ready for the unthinkable.

---

[111] This is actually a very bad way of recovering from hypothermia as it can lead to cardiac arrest as the cold blood from the extremities makes its way to the heart and can cause shock to the heart

This is very much like the Law of the Old Testament. It was a temporary means to teach us. Galatians Chapter 4 calls the Law a "guardian" or if King Jimmy[112] is more your style, a "tutor". The law is a steppingstone to something truly wonderful. It positions us to recognize the cross as the perfection of the law, it reveals the Messiah and the fallacy of self-reliance.

So, to bring this into focus we turn to Romans 4 and discover that Abraham's faith and credited (imputed) righteousness was the original plan for salvation. It clearly proceeds the Law and one might argue it was also the Edenic foundation of people's connection to God. Our ability to understand this original plan was heavily damaged by sin. Think of the Law as traffic cones, a temporary means to bypass the damage done by sin and get us back on the original highway of the supremacy of Christ; trusting Him as Lord, Savior and Teacher, aka a righteousness by faith. The surprise is that the detour doesn't get us back on track, but rather drives us into the ditch, but right in front of the sign that says, "call 911 for a rescue". We need a tow truck to get us back on the highway of faith. We must be rescued, but more importantly, we need to realize we need to be rescued.

Psychologists will tell us that children learn essential life skills through play. Games and play are important means by which we learn. So, let's introduce the idea of the depravity of man. One of the central tenants of this model is that our minds have been affected by sin and we are, in fact, brain damaged. We need a lot of help to learn about the Gospel. This, of course, runs against the grain of those entrenched in the supremacy of self but this will be addressed in a few chapters.

There is little disagreement with the idea that there is a learning curve for individuals. Obviously, adults know more than children, although at times there remains a difficulty in convincing kids of this key factoid. Now let's entertain the idea that there is also a learning curve for cultures and, by extension, a learning curve of history as well. Keep this in mind as we combine a war game in Virginia with the Law found

---

[112] King James Version

in the Old Testament. The Old Testament is often a point of confusion for many contemporary Christ followers.

Enter the Law.

We must be brought to the point where it becomes clearly obvious that we cannot save ourselves, we must depend on someone else to rescue us. In order for us to arrive at this point of realization that we are in fact not OK, several prerequisites must be put in place so our dulled brains can have the "aha!" moment that causes a change.

But to get to this central point, God needed to teach the Jewish people, and by extension, all of humanity, some pivotal points over many generations. So, let's view the OT Law as a means of teaching these points to children through a "game". We are not talking about individuals as children, but the culture and people growing in its understanding of things as God reprograms our collective minds spanning generations. It takes hundreds of years to drill this into our heads. We must learn our ABCs before we can read Shakespeare. There are many things we must learn to get ready for graduation day.

Now remember that our default mindset as a fallen person is to "do something to earn God's approval". This, of course, is our fig leaf mentality. So, God says, "OK give it a whirl." He lays down just 10 commandments, "Do these and you will be OK". He then gives a boatload of lesser commands that could be considered "case law" or specific examples of how each of the 10 play out, this way there is no misunderstanding of the big 10 which is the summation of what is called "The Moral Law".

The Jews wholeheartedly give it a shot, thinking, "we got this" and thinking it is a means to qualify them for God's approval. But let's be clear, the 10 commandments are the bare minimum of moral behavior, and everyone will eventually fail at some point. God confidently knows this and also knows it will ultimately bring the Jews to the unexpected realization that they are actually disqualified; His plan all along.

Now, unbeknownst to the Jews the Law is like quicksand. It works only in one direction: condemnation. Then, to make matters "worse", the more you fight it, the more entrapped you get. There seems to be no win here, but the genius of this strategy is that the Law was given to people who trust in their performance and will drive the humble amongst them, to the realization that a rescue and a new heart[113] is actually what they need. God quietly sits back and watches His plan brilliantly unfold.

Now it needs to be understood that the Old Testament Law is actually broken into three categories, in addition to the Moral Law there is also Civil and Ceremonial law. This is often not delineated as clearly as a western thinker might want them to be, but keep in mind that not everybody thinks like a westerner either.

The Civil Law, which we would call "criminal law" is a means by which human courts mirror the coming judgment day of The Lord. People are accountable to a higher authority and the just consequences of prohibited moral actions reflect God's perspective on the matter. This is what we call "justice". Our "conscience" drives us to avoid doing things that are against the Moral Law, and it also creates an internal tension called "guilt" when we disobey. We intuitively know we owe a moral debt. Crime costs the victim dearly and the civil law shows that there is also a corresponding cost to the perpetrator as well. This blunt instrument of human justice is means to get the attention of a self-centered person. Justice offsets any short term gain that sin may offer someone. Justice keeps society from spinning wildly out of control and justice is the last love language to gain the attention of a wayward soul. Things have gone seriously wrong, and a fix is needed, both in the physical world as well as the spiritual.

Enter the sacrifice (Ceremonial Law)

The just debt we owe, our guilt, is the foremost internal indicator within us that we are in a bad standing with people and, by extension, God. Our flawed performance and guilt bring our short comings to the forefront of our self-centered thinking. So, settling this debt is paramount to our self-interest, but it is also clear that there really is no recourse within our abilities for doing this. No amount of "good" can

---

[113] Ezekiel 36:26

erase a “bad”. “I did not shoot the bank teller when I robbed the bank,” does not let the thief off the hook.

The just and massive debt of our sin needs to be dealt with as the mandatory first step. So, God prescribes the Old Testament Ceremonial/Sacrificial Law to teach us this. The only problem is that it didn’t work. Well let me restate that; it didn’t work to take away our sin, but it did work to teach us what needs to be done.[114]

The Sacrificial/Ceremonial Law is the means to teach us the fundamental principles about repairing our shattered relationship with God. The sacrificial part of the Law drives us to two essential points. First and foremost, we are taught that our sin debt is huge, it’s a capital offense, and we cannot pay it. But the real kicker of the sacrifice teaches us that there is an escape clause; I can have someone else pay my debt. The Law, in its entirety, teaches us this and primes us for understanding that the real solution is grace and the cross, the rescue we ultimately need.

The writer of Hebrews reinforces this and teaches us that the animal sacrifices are a recurring reminder of the problem and not the ultimate solution.[115] We go through the motions for centuries, but something is clearly missing, a sacrifice that actually works is clearly needed. The ominous sin debt is our Goliath, taunting us and blocking us from the only way to return to God, he must be slain.

For centuries everything seemed to be in place with the temple and sacrifices, but the giant of sin debt just did not die, even though countless animals were sacrificed. It is clear that a sacrifice is needed, but it needs to be something with actual power behind it.

The uncrossable barrier between people and God, better understood as spiritual death is symbolized by the veil of the Temple, it stubbornly remains for hundreds of years.

---

[114] Salvation under the OT is an involved discussion, the animal sacrifices reflect the trust in the promised of a Messiah in the future, hence faith. Christians in the NT trust in the acts of the Messiah in the past.

[115] Hebrews 10:1-4

We are hopelessly trapped by the Law; Galatians is the go-to book to clarify that the Law is not a means of salvation but rather a means to diagnose our wretched condition before God.

"For if a law had been given that could impart life, then righteousness would certainly have come by the law."[116]

"I do not set aside the grace of God, for if righteousness could be gained through the law, Christ died for nothing!"[117]

"For all who rely on observing the law are under a curse, for it is written: 'Cursed is everyone who does not continue to do everything written in the Book of the Law.' Clearly no one is justified before God by the law, because the righteous will live by faith"[118]

Our obedience to the Law does not save us, but it poises us to see the necessity of someone else saving us, it opens our eyes to grace[119].

Hebrews tells us that the earthly tabernacle was just a copy of the real one in heaven.[120] The role playing of the earthly temple sacrifices taught us what will happen in the real temple when the Messiah intercedes for us and the problem will be dealt with permanently.[121] The blank ammo of the animal sacrifices did not slay the giant, but one shot of live ammo, the cross, did.[122] Therefore we can now step over the carcass of Goliath and slip from this prison of self, and enter the presence of The Living God. Nothing is new except the ammo used,

---

[116] Galatians 3:21

[117] Galatians 2:21

[118] Galatians 3:10-11

[119] Luke 7:29-30

[120] Hebrews 9:24

[121] Hebrews 10:11-14, 7:23-27

[122] Hebrews 9:9-28

the focus is on the cross, the rescue is by the Messiah, not an actual lamb but the very Son of God, THE Lamb of God,[123] the sacrifice that is decisively in another category.

Seconds before death, Jesus declared that "it is finished."[124] Upon His death, the veil was completely torn.[125] The separation between man and God is gone! However, let us be exceptionally clear here; Jesus tore the veil, not us. The cross saves, not our fig leaves. The sinner's prayer of repentance is the ultimate 911 call for rescue. The cross fixes what we cannot. No longer relying on self, our Savior becomes Jesus.

The animal sacrifices of the Old Testament magnificently foreshadowed the day when the Perfect Priest offers the Perfect Sacrifice that is the perfect solution to make people perfect. All this theology sometimes obscures the obvious: we are now reconciled to the Father, he is no longer the angry judge, He is now "Dad".

> *"... but you received the Spirit of sonship. And by him we cry, 'Abba Father.' The Spirit himself testifies with our spirit that we are God's children. Now if we are children, then we are heirs—heirs of God and co-heirs with Christ..."*[126]

We must understand that when Christ became the sacrifice, He personally bore the just penalty of our sin. Voluntarily declining any retribution is the foundation of what is called "forgiveness". Criminal justice does not repair a relationship, but forgiveness does, and it is always by the consent of the injured party, it can never be forced by the offender. The dual cost of sin, the huge damage done to the sinner and the victims of sin was borne by the New High Priest, Jesus, when He offered himself. And this clear act of monumental kindness is not even remotely earned, it was entirely an act of grace. Once it is

---

[123] John 1:29

[124] John 19:30

[125] Matthew 27:51

[126] Romans 8:15-18 "abba" is Aramaic for "dad"

claimed, we stand before the Father not just forgiven, but also righteous. Our connection to Him as His child is permanently restored[127].

But wait, there's more…

God's selfless love for people is clearly demonstrated by the cross, but the animal sacrifices also show that another death is required, our death. Romans 12 shows the proper response to the cross is one of a "living sacrifice". We die to self as a natural response of Christ dying for us. Being selfless is paramount to bearing the image of God because the Trinity is the ultimate expression of this selflessness. This dying to self mindset unleashes the Holy Spirit to transform our lives. Self has to get out of the way, and we need that new heart.

All this so The Father can bring back to life His precious children who have been lost. The cost of sin is huge, the cost to fix it is, likewise, huge and like I said before, everyone must die to make this right. The death of a lamb points us to this.

Often it is said that the Old Testament is "obsolete". It is better understood that the Sacrificial Law is "fulfilled."[128] The escape clause of a new and permanent High Priest, and the Perfect Sacrifice made the animal sacrifices pointless. They were just blanks, ineffective but instructive.

I have only played war games and never fired a shot in combat, my sacrifice for this country is but a chipped front tooth. I am by no means a hero of any sort, but I have talked to those who have been in combat, and they all repeat the same thought: They all paused and contemplated that this is no longer a game but the real deal when live ammo was issued. I think that the OT sacrificial Law was a great means of teaching us that we cannot save ourselves and it also shows us about the champion of the Gospel; Christ Jesus, The Messiah, has

---

[127] 1 John 3:1

[128] Matthew 5:17

ushered in the new era of the New Covenant, a covenant of unbelievably amazing grace.

There only remains one question in my mind about this whole matter; Why could I not learn this lesson on a warm summer night?

THE LAKE

On the campus of SUNY Oswego, in upstate New York, there are two special locations that hold special significance to me. If permission would be granted, I would erect monuments on those two spots to mark them because of the magnitude of what was revealed to me at these locations. The first one really doesn't need a monument since there is a large ash tree growing there that will suffice for a marker. This is where I responded to God's whispered invitation for salvation, "Now or never, choose tonight". The Father assured me of His love and that all would be forgiven if I embraced the cross. My understanding of theology was near zero. What my life would look like in the future was also unknown. What mattered was that the whisper came from a God who loved me and it was to this God that I said "Yes". To the outside observer this makes no sense, it is not rational. Even to me, a low emotional, critical thinker, it cannot be justified by reason, but I would liken it to responding to a very familiar and trusted voice that I never audibly heard. 40+ years later I have zero regrets.

There is no way the State of New York would allow a monument on the second spot because it is on a sidewalk. I would want a very large stone, proportional to the magnitude of revealed truth, but they would scream and holler about blocking pedestrian traffic, snow removal impedance and maintenance costs, so I do not even ask because the answer will be "No". This is called the chain drop spot. Within a few months of salvation, a simple truth turbo charged my life and there was now no turning back. This revelation involved a large body of water called Lake Ontario.

What appeared to happen at the lake that summers day at a CMA[129] church camp seemed ordinary. My recollection is that it was a pleasant day, with burgers on the BBQ and being surrounded by my new church family. It made for a very enjoyable day; ideal might be a better word that would sum things up. But the festive picnic atmosphere of the physical world did not reflect the enormity of the events happening in the spiritual realm. There are things that happen in this unseen world during baptism that are very real but undiscovered by most folks. Satan's teeth are knocked out and our enemy stands on the precipice of a barrier that he cannot cross but we can. He stands powerless as his prisoner is finally unlocked from his control and taken to safety on the other side. Enraged, he can now only shout across the waters of baptism and lob the occasional arrow. The battle has changed, and he has lost. His only play to keep control over you, is the hope that you will fail to realize that you are truly free. Death to self, and the waters of baptism, have freed the captive.

Like many who are rescued from the darkness, we carry wounds into our new lives. Redemption and forgiveness are instantaneous at salvation, but now the process of restoration, healing and rehabilitation begins. This process is ultimately customized to each person by Jesus, The Great Physician.[130] He knows exactly what needs to be done and in what order they need to be done. He ultimately involves His people to join Him in this work so we can share in His joy as we deeply invest in the lives of people. The two physician's aides that came to my side were Paul Shiffer and John Robinson. Paul was a student leader and John was the Navigator Staff at SUNY Oswego.

---

[129] Christian and Missionary Alliance Church

[130] Jeremiah 30:17 Luke 5:31

There were a lot of things I needed to learn about my Heavenly Father and both Paul and John were excellent teachers. Their knowledge of God's Word was impressive, but more importantly, they lived it. The fatal hemorrhaging wound that followed me was a deeply rooted pain that was the result of aggressive rejection by people. Being on the life-long receiving end of rejection and abuse certainly does not build up a person's self-esteem and thus the need becomes greater, and when the need becomes greater, the rejection becomes more frequent, severe and assured. Thus, into the powerful spiral of despair I sank. It was from this darkness that I was saved. Being relationally illiterate, I had nothing to offer anyone who might befriend me. I was a black hole of need. As an unsaved person, when this deficit was discovered, it was a friendship deal breaker for everybody. But even as a new Christian, I was in danger of bleeding out from this wound in short order, but Paul and John rushed in to give me first aid.

The focus of so much ministry these days seems to be focused on teaching the neophyte about the Bible. Since this is basically my role in the church I can wholeheartedly endorse it. Jesus Himself prayed to the Father that His followers would be sanctified by the truth, "your Word is truth."[131] It is amazing to me how many believers' crash and burn because of lack of understanding of some basic Biblical truth. Christianity is not rocket surgery, but simple basic truths seem to be misunderstood or unknown by the masses. Our enemy shouts lies across the water. Our defense is Biblical truth. Some lessons are learned by reading and discussion, others need to be demonstrated, and character of course, needs to be modeled. The academics of the Bible are certainly important, but there is more to discipleship than the "academics". It is helpful when someone is by your side and says, "hear that voice?" It's a lie."

I stumbled into the Kingdom, smoldering from the battle and hit hard with the shrapnel of sin. I think the timing of my arrival surprised most. But Paul and John applied a tourniquet to the wounds that threatened to bleed me out. They accepted me along with my new church family, but these two guys that invested in me and were able to pass on their knowledge of God's truth and the reality of knowing Him. Remember,

---

[131] John 17:17

I brought nothing to the friendship table, yet they extended the right hand of fellowship to me. This belonging, this inclusion, being invited, and greeted, made all the difference in the world to me.

Helping others that cannot pay you back is a clear demonstration of unconditional agape' love that is the very nature of the Living God. In a nutshell, this is called grace. Paul and John, themselves restored, paid it forward and lived lives of healing others. Their joy and reward immense, they are examples to follow. Connected to Christ the vine, the source, they were a conduit of blessing to people in need, and I was a person with a heap load of need. They were Jesus with skin on, and the Spirit worked through them. Their connection to Jesus was the foundation for their effect on others, and it was profound.

The lie that my enemy shouted across the lake was that I was not loved by God and His people; a familiar line to my ears. Having heard this continuously for years, I was conditioned to believe it even though the evidence was to the contrary. My abandoned but familiar flotsam of despair and withdrawal was pushed across the waters by the enemy. It drifted close by, "Remember this? It is your only safe place." was the lie of the enemy. John was insightful to helping me understand my predisposition to be controlled by this legacy. My current situation was that I was very much a product of my past and struggled relentlessly with it. The key here is knowing and understanding that although this is indeed an extremely powerful force, things were about to change significantly.

After the euphoria of a new life settled down, the doubts came on in full force. The armies of the darkness were dispatched and caught up with me. Satan yelled lies to me from across the water and I struggled deeply with this familiar voice from the shadows. I was walking along the sidewalk one day wrestling with this dilemma. "Was I a prisoner of my past?" A new life is what I signed up for and now I question would this wound ever be healed. Then, once again, the King of Kings and Lord of Lords whispered to my spirit a very simple truth, "By the way Kurt, I am greater than your past". A combination of understanding His Word and a clear demonstration of agape love from my two mentors brought me to the response, "Yes you are". Satan could no longer yank my chain from across the lake, the chains fell off. The penalty of sin was broken by the finished work of the cross, but now also its power. My walk with Christ, although with a limp, moves me further from the shore of the waters that Satan cannot cross. He can only shout from the far side. This journey's key event was an enjoyable day on the lake.

We read in Exodus how God's people were delivered from slavery in Egypt thousands of years ago. It is still celebrated every year by the Jews with the observance of the Passover. The parallels of the cross and the Passover are nothing short of astounding, a worthy study of all Christians. But the deliverance was two staged to the careful reader.

After the shock of the death of all the first born in Egypt, the Egyptians did not simply let the Hebrew slaves go, they begged them to go. They were so eager to see them go, they gave them gold, silver and livestock to send them on their way.[132] However, a few days later they had a change of heart. Motivated by the need to get their slaves back, the armies of darkness were dispatched to pursue the newly released Hebrews.[133] We read that the Israelites were cornered by Pharaoh's army at the Red Sea. A military super power versus a rag tag bunch of ex slaves. Certain defeat of the Jews was at hand. Then the familiar miracle of the parting of the Red Sea takes place. The Israelites escape through the waters and got to the other side. Once there, Pharoah's army then advanced into the still parted sea. I would assume that the soldiers were probably freaked out by these rather unusual circumstances. I know I would have at least snapped a selfie to capture the moment, but nevertheless, the Egyptians also attempted to cross. But before they emerged on the other side, the walls of water came crashing down and obliterated them.[134] This barrier of water where we die to self, die to sin and die to the law, cannot be crossed by the powers of darkness. These are the waters

---

[132] Exodus 12:31-36

[133] Exodus 14:5-9

[134] Exodus 14:26-31

of baptism and, in my case, were the waters of Lake Ontario.

"Give me a verse!", some people rightfully shout. Is this a legitimate Biblical parallel? Paul calls the crossing of the Red Sea a baptism in 1 Corinthians 10:2:

> *"They (the Jews that escaped Egypt) were all baptized into Moses in the cloud and in the (Red) sea."*

So, what happened in the unseen spiritual world that fine summer day on the shores of Lake Ontario? We turn to Romans chapter 6 for further understanding. In baptism we are formally united with Christ in His death and raised to newness of life. The original power play by the enemy in Eden is to get us to decide to live for self. Every subsequent move of the enemy relies on this prerequisite mindset of pride; thus, we are controlled by these chains of the enemy. Live for self and the shackles work, we are slaves, but die to self and the shackles fall off, we are free, the lies of the enemy simply don't work anymore.

Obviously, the reality of this freedom lies on a spectrum. The more you die to self, the more the power of sin is broken in your life. The more you comprehend grace, the more you die to self. The one-time event of water baptism clearly declares the central point of the Gospel; reliance on the cross as opposed to reliance on doing good. Baptism represents a giant leap forward on this spectrum and has repercussions that are categorically profound in the spirit world, even though we only get wet in the physical. We are irrevocably united with Christ in His death and also irrevocably united with His resurrection. We die to the law, pardons are issued, adoptions finalized, and contracts become null and void .[135] All sorts of stuff seems to key off of this event, and it happened to me one pleasant day at a Bible camp on the shores of Lake Ontario. Every mature Christian I know has been water baptized, and many who struggle in the faith have never taken this step.

The difference between a baptized believer and a non-baptized one seems to be which side of the Red Sea you are on. Are you locked in

---

[135] Romans 7:1-4

combat, tooth and nail with the enemy or is he shooting arrows from a distance? Like a cat in a tree, the dog cannot follow, but in our case, Satan cannot swim. He has no direct hold on the forgiven who have died to self and passed through the waters of baptism.

Time to decide which side of the Red Sea to be on. If you are a believer, you have died to self, died to sin and died to the law, it is high time that the corpse gets buried. If you are still on the wrong side of the sea, it is time to get baptized and cross to the other side where you can escape the direct powers of the enemy. Breaking the back of sin's power is not a testament to human resolve. God parted the Red Sea, not Moses. Uniting myself with the death and resurrection of Christ via baptism, likewise, makes me but a passenger on this incredible trip from one side of the sea to the other. But make no mistake, this is a one-way ticket. Now truly free, the journey to the Promised Land begins.

God has taken decades to show me a fuller understanding of the Gospel. Mind blowing barely describes it. My writing ability, I assure you, does not do justice to the magnificence of the Gospel. This incredible story, revealed in Scripture and demonstrated in the lives of hundreds of people I have come to know is the foundation of assurance that my life is based on.

This is very obvious to me, but why is it not clear to others? The answer is found in what theologians call "the depravity of man". A lesson late one night on a beach in California provides the perfect analogy.

THE COP

It was a tough decision whether to flee from the cop or do what he said. He approached me as I emerged from the surf on a California beach late one summer night; I kept my distance from him as he demanded that I produce some ID. I was guilty by association only; wrong place, wrong time and I had no ID on me. I insisted that I was not drunk and did nothing wrong, I arguably just saved some one's life. However, for each step he took forward, I took one step back to keep my distance, again stating that I had done nothing wrong. He grew more insistent and demanded compliance.

At that time, I was a lieutenant in the US Marine Corps, a trip to the local cop shop would not have a good outcome, but I had one key asset to my advantage; I could run a sub five-minute mile[136] and there was nothing but open beach at hand. Only track stars and Olympians could match my fleetness of feet. No disrespect intended, but I did not think this local peace officer was either. Being misunderstood and misinterpreted most of my life, I have a keen sixth sense of when

---

[136] My experience is that 1/100 of 1% of people can break a 5 minute mile

things can go very wrong, and this was such a time. Any use of force in this situation was out of the question; get screwed or run. He took a few quick steps towards me, attempting to take control of the situation, and I bolted: game on.

My skill set and conditioning instantly kicked in. At that time in my life, I had many glaring deficits in my life but as stated, running fast and far was by no means one of them. I did a decent 100-meter sprint, holding back just a bit, just in case I had to play the card I could destroy everyone with, distance. I glanced behind me to reassess the situation, he was nowhere in sight, clearly outclassed he didn't even make an attempt at this contest. Reasonably secure, I used my Marine Corps escape and evade training to get back to my car. I then left the area, mission accomplished, minus some old running shoes and a shirt. It's a messy world and sometimes there are no perfect outcomes, but this night was a perfect lesson about the depravity of man.

As I have already stated, I hate parties and that night we had an officer's call at a fellow lieutenant's apartment just off base and close to the beach. This time it was just for the junior officers. I was going to create the illusion of participation by just showing up late, say "Hi" to a few key folks, eat some food and then slip from the event. I was just about to execute the last phase of my plan when the cops knocked on the door to get us to turn the music down since it was past 10pm. We did not earn any points with the local constables, since the host, along with just about everyone there, were nicely sloshed and somewhat obnoxious towards the cops. We turned down the music and the cops left, but we were now on their radar.

Obviously, to the inebriated mind, the next thing to do since the party was shut down was to run down to the beach and go for a swim. I had heard on the radio earlier that there was a high surf warning in effect for the next few days. Drunk people, high surf and the dead of night are not a good combination in my book, so instead of leaving, I tagged along to play lifeguard, being amongst the few that were sober. What we are doing redlines the stupid meter, but I was compelled by loyalty to keep an eye on my comrades, so I tagged along.

Loud and proud, we raised quite a ruckus on the way, as we sang Marine Corps "jodys"[137] at the top of our lungs as we double timed in formation down to the nearby beach. There was no doubt that the locals of this quiet beachside community would call 911 and complain, that there were "A bunch of drunk Marines at the beach".

The group took a short swim and then started to reassemble to go back to the house. I stood next to the host as we tried to account for everyone in the moonlight. Unfortunately, one fellow lieutenant was still in the surf and had decided to swim for Hawaii.

We both saw this and he uttered, "Whiskey tango foxtrot over"[138]

"Roger that," I replied, "I think it's Kelly".

He used his best infantry officer yell to get Kelly's attention but to no avail, Kelly was going deep.

"I'll get him." I said, as I slipped my running shoes and shirt off and dove into the Pacific to retrieve the aforementioned, directionally challenged, officer. Being sober and an accomplished ocean swimmer, I caught up to him quickly. I grabbed his ankle about 100 yards from the shore.

"Kelly, where are you going?" I yelled so I could be heard above the crashing surf.

"Going back to the party… follow me…it'll be fun." He replied.

"You are heading the wrong way."

"Really?...Are you sure?"

"Yeah, I got the G2[139] on this, you're drunk, I'm not."

---

[137] A "jody" is a call and response cadence popular in the military used during marching. Jody is a popular character in such songs and represents a civilian that the military looks down on.

[138] This is the phonetic alphabet used on military radios, specifically WTF?

[139] G2 is the Generals Staff that is responsible for intelligence

“Thanks, Blombo.” and he swam towards the beach, safely headed in the right direction. I swam behind him to make sure he got back to dry land.

There were quite a few cops on the moonlit beach as we arrived, and I was not sensing any level of approval or endearment on their part by their activity and body language. The other guys were scattering but Kelly walked right into the melee. I wanted to avoid this situation. So, I swam to the side of the scene and quietly emerged, but to no avail, an alert cop saw me, and thus the race, if you could call it that, in the sand ensued.

The concept of the depravity of man is often misunderstood; it is actually properly called “the total depravity of man”[140] by theologians. This does not mean that people always max out their sin. Unbelievers are capable of acts of kindness and righteous deeds as we see this all the time. Rather, it postulates that every aspect of our lives has been damaged by sin. As such, one of its key tenets is that people are totally incapable of self-navigating salvation. Dead people cannot do anything to save themselves because they are dead; they need the intervention of a Doctor, EMT etc. to perform CPR and resuscitate them. And so it is with spiritual death; self-saving is impossible, an intervention by someone with life is required.

So, what does spiritual CPR have to do with a foot race against a cop on a California beach? Well, nothing really, but it’s part of the story that illuminates another key part of the depravity of man, it parallels the mindset of the drunk officer trying to swim to Hawaii from a beach in California. Spiritually dead people, like drunks, have grossly impaired judgment, it is impossible for them to figure out how to be rescued. A spiritually and relationally suicidal ideology and life seems to make perfect sense to a depraved mind. Totally wrong, yet totally confidant, is not a good combination, but to Hawaii they swim en masse. Adam had the same problem, he thought the fig leaves

---

[140] This is one of the five points of reformed theology remembered by the mnemonic “TULIP”. The “T” stands for the “Total depravity of man” Google it

worked, but they didn't. The very real depravity of man starts at the moment of the fall and continues to this very day. Our efforts don't work, our brains don't work either; it's called self-deception.

When Jesus asked His disciples, "Who do the people say the Son of Man is?" They shared a mixed bag of spiritual sounding answers; John the Baptist resurrected, one of the prophets etc. Jesus then gets personal, "Who do you say I am?" Peter replied, "You are the Christ, the Son of the Living God"[141]

Jesus was stunned[142] and commented, "Blessed are you, Simon, son of Jonah. For this was not revealed to you by flesh and blood, but by my Father". This passage shows that we cannot escape our depraved self-deception via our own capacity; we need help directly from God. I think we must ask for this and be disposed to embracing the truth when we get it. The prophet Jeremiah penned a key promise of God, "You will seek me and find me, when you seek me with all your heart."[143] I did this, albeit by accident, in the Catskills, but it still worked, God blessed it and showed me the Gospel.

Very few people these days quiet themselves and ask the big questions in life, fewer still ever make the big course corrections in life. Like lemmings, they follow the crowd and go with the flow. Unfortunately, the only fish that always goes with the flow, is a dead fish. I am no spiritual hero in this regard, I did not figure this out. I unwittingly stumbled upon Jeremiah's promise of divine revelation via the anguish of a broken life. It caused me to pray with my whole heart in the Catskills. Realizing that something was very wrong, I instinctively knew I was trapped in the wrong life, but I stubbornly held to my self-destructive course. It made no sense, but welcome to the depravity of man. My prayer of desperation, was simple, "Where are

---

[141] Matthew 16:16-17

[142] OK another editorial insertion here. Jesus' reaction is not recorded in the Bible, but I have a hard time imagining Jesus not at least smiling at this

[143] Jerimiah 29:13

you God? Why is it so painful to be alive?" Misery was God's grace in a strange wrapper... when I opened it, I got revelation. Revelation is a loaded theological term meaning God chose to reveal the Gospel. Hidden in plain sight all along, but unseen due to my blindness. I didn't figure this out, God showed me from His Word. He opened my mind so I could understand the obvious. Repentance and "duh" was my response.

Many years later I got a clearer perspective of the depth of man's depravity. Self-deception is a very destructive force in a proud person's life. For several years I took a night job as an armed guard to earn some extra money. Our company would be a sub-contractor for a local police agency to guard suicidal patients in the hospital. This would allow a sworn officer to get back on the streets instead of "baby sitting" some guy in the hospital. I did this too many times to count and some of these people told me their stories. Every one of them had a common denominator; their life was a lie. They knew it in their spirit, but they shouted it down in their minds as they repeated the same lie over and over again. This is a clear indicator of man's depravity. The tensioned battle inside eventually led to a handful of pills, a bottle of liquor or the ledge of a building. CS Lewis wrote, "God...shouts in our pain. It's his megaphone to rouse a deaf world". The pangs of spiritual death are telling; I know this first hand and I see it in others as well. It's everywhere once you open your eyes to it.

So, what is the key to discerning what camp you are in? "By their fruit you will recognize them."[144] is what Jesus said. The agony of the soul, troubling purposelessness, dysfunctional human relationships and God being a million miles away are but a few clues. Our sense of reality is warped by this filter of pain, and we become impervious to truth as we stubbornly follow a broken compass. A life then drifts wildly off course. You were not created to live this way.

---

[144] Matthew 7:16-20

Intervention by someone with life is the only thing that can save mankind. The very Son of God came down to Earth and showed the world that he was indeed the Son of God with powerful teaching and miracles. After revealing the final secrets of the Gospel, and praying that the ultimate goal of the Gospel, the reconnection of God's people to each other and to Himself be fulfilled.[145] He then executed the pivotal phase of the plan, the cross. Then, three days later to show His befuddled followers that it worked, He rose from the grave, definitively demonstrating the absolute victory over humanity's biggest problem: death, both spiritual and physical death wiped out in a single blow.[146] Then from Pentecost to today all who trust the cross and trust the grace of God, enjoy a life changing Spirit to spirit relationship with the Father and a deep sense of belonging to the community of believers, the life we were ultimately created for.

Rely on self and the lie of self-salvation by good deeds is what we hold on to. Even though the power of sin defeats us in life, we foolishly and unswervingly hold to this dead-end approach. The internal tension should get our attention, but it does not. This irrational dichotomy illuminates the depravity of man. Die to self and the truth of the cross is clear. "God opposes the proud but gives grace to the humble[147]".

Step back and compare, look at the big picture of religious leaders, both past and present. Boil it down and sift through the religious babble and see that all offer a solution of salvation by good deeds. Peddlers of fig leaves they are, the whole lot of them. Christianity, on the other hand, is fundamentally different. Salvation by grace, it is in a category by itself. All award winning religious leaders of the past; Buddha, Mohammed, Joseph Smith, Krishna, all remain in their graves. Virtually all have the common thread of reliance on something you do or something you know. Christians have an empty grave, and

---

[145] John 17:20-23

[146] 1 Corinthians 15:54-56

[147] James 4:6 NIV 1984

they speak on behalf of the one that has conquered death; The Risen Christ.

I am betting everything on the empty grave.

Others have concluded that "God is dead" it has a nice ring to it and many people rally to it and are suckered completely by its accompanying rhetoric. Christians, understanding the significance of this issue, quickly retort, "God's not dead, He is alive!" To my dear brethren I would advise, "Not so fast." The fact is, that the atheist is close to being spot on from a Biblical perspective. However, I propose a somewhat different response to the atheist, "Actually, you are affirming what the Bible says, except that God's not dead....rather, you are." When we understand this in light of the depravity of man, then the Christian can be used to give life to the spiritually dead.

To the unbelievers who read this; ask yourself; is a Christian, a spokesperson for the author of life and the vanquisher of death, grabbing you by the ankle and trying to rescue you? Come and see that by a simple clipping into the rescue plan of the cross, all is solved and a mind is reprogrammed. Everything hinges on who is supreme. Lord and Savior self or Lord and Savior Jesus? Who has an empty grave?

A sincere prayer of "God rescue me" primes people to receive the truth of God's Word. But one must be predisposed to being rescued from a life of sin rather than just the consequences there of. A mindset of "I got this," is way off the mark and is a tried and true formula for living a delusional life, that is bench marked by the collateral damage pride inflicts on self and others. A turtle drives this point home.

THE TURTLE

There are only a few things that cause me to question God's wisdom; one of them is the snapping turtle. Truly a hideously looking, ill-tempered, cold-blooded beast, the antithesis of cuddly, his only redeeming quality is that he makes good soup.

My wife was born and raised on the prairie of North Dakota and while visiting the family farm one summer the whole gang decided to fish a slow-moving creek in order to get a stringer full of catfish. You see mom has a killer recipe and all of us were itching for a catfish lunch.

My wife's rod bends almost to the point of breaking and we first thought she just hooked into the likes of a sunken tree branch, but after several minutes, she pulls to the surface this mini-monster befit for an alien sci-fi movie. I, of course, with the degree in zoology instantly recognized the local representative of the Chelydridae family and jumped into the knee-deep water to grab the 20-pound beast by its tail and throw him onto the bank. After the "oohs" and "aahs" associated with encountering such a strange critter, the group think instantly concluded that turtle soup was to be added to the lunch menu, so into the back of the pickup he went.

When we returned to the farm house, we handed the catfish over to mom who went about preparing them in accordance with her favorite recipe. The brothers and I were left with the task of figuring out how to reduce an angry snapping turtle to soup meat. Step one was the chopping block. Every farm has one and the chickens seemed relieved that after we got the hatchet sharpened, none of their friends started squawking. Safe for the day they went about scratching the dirt and attended to issues that are pressing in the chicken world. The turtle for some reason seemed uncooperative about this phase of the operation. I exploited his namesake patented move and teased him with a short branch about an inch in diameter. He obliged with a lightning-fast snap and a vise like grip on the branch with his very powerful jaws. The tug of war ensued, in which a 200-pound man easily won and the turtle's neck was stretched out for the deed, he never saw it coming.

It was not surprising that the turtle's jaws remained tightly clamped on the branch. Reptiles are notoriously slow to die even after decapitations. Many ER doctors will tell you that a good percentage of snake bite victims have been bitten by "dead" snakes. These are snakes that have been shot, stomped on, whacked with garden implements etc. and when picked up to be thrown away, the disposer gets bitten by the disposed.

I hung the branch in a tree with the turtle's head still clamped onto it, gently swinging in the breeze. I turned my attention to the matter at hand; preparation of our reptilian dinner guest. After some improvised techniques involving power saws, hammers, pry bars and knives we reduced him to small cubes of meat. It was a point of surprise that his heart was still beating when we scrapped him off the cutting board into the soup pot. Nevertheless after some home-grown root vegetables and various spices, the turtle soup and fried catfish were enjoyed by all.

After lunch, I walked out onto the porch for proper digestion and observed that the turtle's head was still gently swinging in the breeze. Surely rigor mortis has set in at this time and a version of turtle lockjaw has produced what I am looking at. Moved by scientific curiosity, I approached the specimen for closer examination.

Hunters will poke downed game in the eye to determine if an animal is truly dead or not; a blinkless response indicates that the game has been reduced to possession. So I used this time-tested technique and to my surprise the turtle blinked, and was still alive! After more than an hour past soup time, Mr. T still had his vise like, tenacious grip on this branch. Unfortunately, I was distracted by other activities of the day, and I was unable to document the exact time for the decapitated turtle, branch gripping, world record that Guinness surely would have been interested in.

Rooted in pride and faith in self, the entrapment of man is fueled by self-supremacy, self-reliance and self-deception. This perfect trifecta of spiritual depravity and deception makes the bondage of man absolute. This strategy works so well, it is page one in the playbook of the enemy. Refusing to let go of works righteousness and pride, like lemmings we plunge from the cliff en masse and drown in the prison of self. Our stubborn, vise-like grip on this errant theology completely blinds us, thus we become like the turtle; we do not realize that we are, in fact, already dead.

The question boils down to trust. Who are we ultimately trusting in? The sin of self-supremacy caused the fall and self-reliance keeps us there. Self-deception seals the deal as we are blinded to God's love and grace, and ultimately to God's solution of the cross. We need God to intervene, to break us out of this cycle where both captive and captor are self.

This trap that has ensnared us, however, can be undone, it's called repentance. Our new life with The Father starts with humble repentance for salvation. Here the Law shows us we have a hell bound problem. It is in our self-interest that this problem be dealt with. We correctly recognize that we cannot trust in ourselves for the fix, thus we are compelled to trust in someone else. Thus, the cycle of self is cracked with reliance on Christ's Sufficiency and the greatest act of selfless love; the cross. Christ's Supremacy soon takes over as we yield to His lordship and finally settle in to have Him as our lifelong Teacher. All to restore us to a life of selflessly loving others, the original plan. John the Baptist sums it up best, "He must become greater and I must become less."[148] Boil all this down and "God opposes the proud but gives grace to the humble[149]".

We worship Jesus as Supreme Lord and Savior with everything we think, say and do. Now worship and humility is not degrading of oneself (for we are created in His image), but rather it's a life that entirely relies on the cross and the imputed righteousness that the Gospel offers. A life of worship, a life truly realigned with the will of the Father, is simply the inherent response and natural consequence to this overwhelming grace. We should naturally reflect our created purpose of bearing the image of God. We can be restored to the imago dei via the cross.

Again, we return to Romans Chapter 12 to understand how we should respond to this revelation of the supre macy of Christ.

> *"Therefore… in view of God's mercy to offer your bodies as a living sacrifice holy and pleasing to God, this is your spiritual act of worship…. Then you will be able to test and approve of what God's will is, His good pleasing and perfect will."*[150]

This simple point bears repetition; an understanding of God's mercy propels us to die to self (living sacrifice) and live a lifestyle of worshipping God. Note the me less supreme, God more supreme exchange. Thrice now we revisit Paul's summary perspective of the big picture:

> *"I have been crucified with Christ and I no longer live, but Christ lives in me. The life I live in the body, I live by faith in the Son of God who loved me and gave himself for me"*[151]

Time for a big picture summary of the entire Bible.

---

[148] John 3:30

[149] James 4:6 NIV 1984

[150] Romans 12:1-2

[151] Galatians 2:20

Decide to live for self and your connection with God is severed and your relationships with people torpedoed. Trying to undo the damage with what you do, makes everything worse, yet you think this is the solution. Your guilt is covered by fig leaves, this approach is worthless.

Decide to rely on the cross and your relationship with God and people is restored. Dying to self daily, you abide in Christ deeper and deeper becoming more like the selfless loving God. Truth is revealed to such people and you are righteous by the cross. This is of immeasurable value.

Live for self and die; die to self and live. 100% nonsense to the lost, 100% certainty to the saved. As Jesus summarized:

> *"The man who loves his life will lose it, while the man who hates his life in this world will keep it for eternal life"*[152]

Jesus came to serve, not to be served and to give his life a ransom for many[153]. Our response to this selfless love is the proverbial two-way street; die for Him. It is a reordering of things in light of the original plan, a repentance for salvation and a dying to self in order to truly live. In prison escape terms: get outside the fence, then run. Theologians refer to this as justification and sanctification.

It is easy for a religious person to hold to a theology of works that cannot save. It is also easy for a saved Christian to hold to an aberrant theology that cannot transform, both are polluted with pride and fig leaves. The tell is simple; dysfunctional relationships with people reflect a dysfunctional relationship with God. Exploring this in appropriate detail will take another book, however, keep this in mind and be aware that the spiritually dead walk among us. Make sure you are not one of them.

---

[152] John 12:25

[153] Mark 10:45

Wow, there is certainly a lot that you can learn from a bowl of turtle soup.

THE VINE

Perhaps my favorite character of the Old Testament is Solomon. I really enjoy his life story and I love the Proverbs. However, when I first encountered his book Ecclesiastes, I was thrown for a loop. It could be argued that the tone of the book is downright suicidal. Solomon's first pitch is a curve ball, he introduces the entire book with:

"Meaningless! Meaningless!"
says the Teacher.
"Utterly meaningless!
Everything is meaningless."[154]

Now that is hardly the perspective one would expect from the wisest person in history. And I will confess that for the first five times I read the book, I genuinely questioned whether or not it was canon.[155]

---

[154] Ecclesiastes 1:2-3

[155] "Canon" is the theological term for the officially included books of the Bible

Chapter after chapter he goes through his life and his accomplishments and categorically declares everything "meaningless

The context of Solomon's life is everything here.

For the record, Solomon was hands down, the ultimate "who's who" in history. He was the powerful King of Israel, rich beyond comprehension, a brainiac of epic repute, built God's Temple, had a reign of peace, had the finest horses, and he was credited with great accomplishments of public works. Thus, he was admired by his subjects, honored by other kings, and sought after for his legendary wisdom. Then topping it off, he had 700 wives and 300 concubines, and I am sure most of those gals fell into the stunningly beautiful category.

Cars, cash and cuties, as my mentor John Robinson would say. This guy was Bill Gates, Hugh Hefner, Elvis, Elon Musk, Einstein and George Washington combined. Everybody on the planet and everyone in history wants to be him. He was absolutely everything that everyone ultimately strives to be. Even to this day, just about everyone is convinced that if they have success in just one of these categories, they will be happy. Solomon maxed out every one of them, so it behooves us to pay attention to his conclusion of the matter.

Then it hit me and Ecclesiastics went from "Is it canon?" to "Oh my God this is amazing." You see, God uses Solomon to definitively answer, once and for all, the eternal question of "What is the meaning and purpose of life?". Every human ultimately contemplates this essential question. Ecclesiastes unequivocally answers it.

Now keep in mind that no one would respect Solomon's conclusion unless it was based on actual experience. So, to conclusively answer THE most important question, God decides, OK, on top of the supernatural wisdom that Solomon prayed for, I will give him everything people think will give them meaning and purpose in life and we will see how it works out for him[156]. People tend to focus on deficits; to wit: "If only I had _________, I would be happy". Solomon filled in every one of those blanks and then some, but still in Chapter 2 he said, "I hated life"[157].

We have a serious disconnect here.

It's mind boggling, and 100% counterintuitive. How can someone who had so much say such a thing? But when we study his life, we see that he slowly drifted from God[158] his life focus shifted. His devotion to God was slowly polluted by the obsessions of the world. When we understand this, only then can we understand the enigma of Ecclesiastes, and only then can we understand the meaning and purpose of life. This unbelievably important lesson still rings true today, but it actually only sets the stage for an even bigger truth that Jesus will slam dunk. But back to Solomon to lay the foundation of things to come.

So, let's summarize Solomon.

From amazing and immersive experience and in 20/20 hindsight, he musters all of his God given over the top, uber wisdom and then looks back on his life and writes the Book of Ecclesiastes. Solomon pens for all time and for all of humanity the irrefutable answer to the question of the meaning and purpose of life:

Now that is hardly the summary perspective one would expect from the wisest person in history. And I will confess that for the first five times I read the book, I seriously questioned whether or not it was canon156. [156] Paraphrasing 1 Kings 3:5-15

[157] Ecclesiastes 2:17

[158] See 1 Kings 11

"Now all has been heard;
here is the conclusion of the matter:
Fear God and keep his commandments,
for this is the whole duty of man.
For God will bring every deed into judgment,
including every hidden thing,
whether it is good or evil."[159]

We better pay attention to this. In a nutshell "Fear God (respect) and keep His commandments."

Ultimately, we are accountable to the God of the Universe and the only thing that matters is a proper relationship to Him. He is not to be trifled with. Thus, our status before God is undeniably the foundation to everything in life, EVERYTHING. This relationship is the marrow of our existence. We were created to be connected to Him, to bear His image and act in love on His behalf. Conforming our lives to the will of the Father overrides everything. He is supreme, not us. His purpose for our lives is paramount, not our goals. We obey Him, He does not obey us. It's not about accomplishments, it's about our connection to our Creator. Without this issue settled, everything else in life becomes utterly meaningless.

Enter Jesus.

The New Testament states that "now someone greater than Solomon is here."[160] Solomon's masterpiece is but a stepping stone to a far greater truth.

Jesus, mirroring Solomon, likewise summarizes everything at the culmination of his earthly life. Hours before His death, the last parable

---

[159] Ecclesiastes 12:13-14

[160] Matthew 12:42

that he gives His disciples was the Parable of the Vine found in John Chapter 15. Pay attention, this is, I would argue, the very culmination of the Scriptures, the essence of the Gospel, the foundational truth to the meaning and purpose of life.

Early in my Christian walk I memorized the entire Parable of the Vine verbatim. For some inexplicable reason this parable jumped off the page. My brain has thus been marinated by this parable for over 40 years. The often-repeated key word in this parable is "remain" ("abide" in other translations). It appears some 11 times in the passage. I would submit that this single word summarizes the big picture of the Scriptures and represents what we are restored to, our original status and our created purpose of image bearers of God. So then, when we are like a fish out of water, the imperative is to return to the relational realm we were created for and then after being returned to a proper grace based, connection to the Risen Christ, remain there and thrive.

Our status before God is often described as a "relationship", a "standing', or a "covenant", all good terms, but reflect only a partial concept. Jesus takes it up a few notches and calls it "remain" and likens it to the permanent connection that a branch has with the trunk of a vine (unity). The central truth is simple; once properly connected to Christ, life flows from the trunk through the branch and creates fruit. Disconnected, the branch does not bear fruit and the branch dies. Branches cannot live and function apart from the vine, they are created to be connected. This connection is 100% based on grace. Replace the 11 times that the word "remains" appears with a permanent grace-based relationship to Christ and the entirety of Scripture makes sense.

It is natural to expect a fish out of water to thrive when it returns to the sea. It is likewise natural to expect a Christian to "bear much fruit" when properly connected to Christ via grace. John records how Jesus succinctly summarizes this relational principle; connection produces fruit, disconnection produces nothing. It's not complicated.

"I am the vine; you are the branches. If a man remains in me and I in him, he will bear much fruit; apart from me you can do nothing"[161]

The central question then is; what does it mean to "remain in Him"? The parable further illuminates that a grace-based connection to Christ is indicated by a restored life of "loving God and loving people". Thus, the parable answers this question; selfless obedience.

Jesus continues,

"As the Father has loved me, so have I loved you. Now remain in my love. If you obey my commands, you will remain in my love, just as I have kept my Father's commands and remain in his love."[162]

Just as Solomon summarizes our connection to God as obedience, Jesus likewise breaks it down for us as obedience. Jesus parallels His connection with the Father to our connection with Him. A life aligned with the will of the Father is clearly not only a selfless response to God's grace, but also an observable indicator of a proper grace-based connection to Christ. The supreme being in our lives is Christ not self, the very essence of humility vs pride. But obey what?

"My command is this: Love each other as I have loved you. Greater love has no one than this: that he lay down one's life for his friends."[163]

The selfless, grace based, divine love that The Father has for His Son is the exact same love that we are to have for others. This singular point represents the restoration of the purpose of our creation; to bear His image and love others on God's behalf does. Boil it down to just

---

161 John 15:5-8

162 John 15:9

163 John 15:13

four words; "love God, love people". Jesus irrefutably demonstrates this big picture of love by then going to the cross. Both spiritual and physical death shatter the relationships we were created for, both deaths wiped out in a single blow. Absolutely, positively we did not earn this, but like a parent doing anything to save a child, the Father and the Son give up everything to save the kids. We can return to the spiritual realm we were created for, a Spirit to spirit, grace based, relationship with our heavenly Father and, likewise grace based connections with people. In the few hours remaining before the end of His physical life, Jesus prays that the cross will deliver just that. Memorize these verses, this is why Jesus paid the price.

> *"My prayer is not for them alone. I pray also for those who will believe in me through their message, that all of them may be one, Father, just as you are in me and I am in you. May they also be in us so that the world may believe that you have sent me. I have given them the glory that you gave me, that they may be one as we are one. I in them and you in me—May that they may be brought to complete unity to let the world know that you sent me and have loved them even as you have loved me."*[164]

This communion with the Father, Son, Spirit and each other is what we were created for, it is offered to us on a silver platter via the cross.

Decades of painful lessons illuminates very clearly one of the great summary verses of the Gospel that reflects this spiritual reality. It is found in Paul's letter to the Church in Ephesus:

> *"For it is by grace you have been saved, through faith—and this is not from yourselves, it is the gift of God, not by works, so that no one can boast. For we are God's workmanship, created in Christ Jesus to do*

---

[164] John 17:20-23

good works, which God prepared in advance for us to do." [165]

It's a gift, not earned, but given so that you can live the life of good works (fruit) that you are supposed to live. Such a great opportunity! Egregious if squandered, extraordinary if seized.

The ramifications of this grace are incalculable.

Scream and holler all you want about being "good", but, to the careful student of the Scriptures, obedience in no way qualifies you for God's acceptance, rather, obedience indicates a life properly connected to Jesus by grace. Same words, different order. Obedience for the right reason is paramount. The totality of the Scriptures can be understood through this lens of grace and the blindfold of pride. Only then is the central truth of Scripture in focus. Solomon in his prophetic wisdom penned these words reflecting this central point thousands of years ago:

"He (God) mocks proud mockers, but gives grace to the humble" [166]

James, the brother of Jesus, requotes Solomon a thousand years later and tweaks it a bit, he summarizes the big picture…

"God opposes the proud, but gives grace to the humble" [167]

The supremacy of self vs the supremacy of Christ.

My escape from the toxic fig leaves of religion revolves around decades of learning focused on the central Biblical doctrine of grace.

---

[165] Ephesians *2:8-10*

[166] Proverbs 3:34

[167] James 4:6

I am broken by how long it took me to grasp this and how many painful mistakes and head injuries were required to bear some modicum of resemblance to His image.

A grace-based connection with the Risen Christ and a grace-based connection with people is all I have now. This foundation intact, the trickle-down details of incorporating grace in day to day living and practice is an all-encompassing endeavor and requires another book to document.[168] For now, I leave you with the hope and prayer that the Apostle Paul starts and ends every one of his letters with:

"Grace be onto you"

---

[168] I'm working on this

Made in USA - Kendallville, IN
16244_9798344395456
11.08.2024 2037